YOUNG
WINSTONE

YOUNG
WINSTONE

RAY WINSTONE

AND BEN THOMPSON

CANONGATE
Edinburgh · London

Published in Great Britain in 2014 by Canongate Books Ltd,
14 High Street, Edinburgh EH1 1TE

www.canongate.tv

1

British Library Cataloguing-in-Publication Data
A catalogue record for this book is available on
request from the British Library

ISBN 978 1 78211 242 6
Export ISBN 978 1 78211 243 3

Typeset in Bembo by Canongate Books Ltd

Printed and bound in Great Britain by Clays Ltd, St Ives plc

CONTENTS

Introduction   VII

Map of Ray Winstone's London   X

1. Hackney Hospital   1

2. Caistor Park Road, Plaistow   12

3. Portway School   23

4. The Odeon, East Ham   32

5. The New Lansdowne Club   41

6. The Cage, Spitalfields Market   50

7. Ronan Point   58

8. Raymond's Tailors, Lower Clapton   66

9. The Repton Boxing Club   75

10. Chrisp Street Market, Poplar   84

11. The Boleyn Ground, Upton Park   93

12. Victoria Park Lido   102

13. The Theatre Royal, Stratford East   112

14. York Hall   122

15. The Prospect of Whitby, Wapping   130

16. Nashville's, Whitechapel   141

17. Benjy's Nightclub, Mile End   153

18. The 277 Bus up Burdett Road   164

19. Gatsby House   175

20. The Alexandra Tavern   184

21. The Tate & Lyle Sugar Factory, Silvertown   195

22. Hackney Marshes   206

23. The Corner of Well Street and Mare Street   217

24. Trossachs, Barking Road   228

25. The Apollo Steakhouse, Stratford   240

Picture credits   251

INTRODUCTION

It's early 2007 and I'm standing on a ship off the coast of north-eastern Australia. We're moored right by Lizard Island, named by my fellow Londoner and Great Briton Captain Cook, and I'm making this film called *Fool's Gold* starring Matthew McConaughey, Kate Hudson and my old mate Donald Sutherland, who is a blinding geezer.

Donald is playing an Englishman and I'm playing a Yank, but in hindsight we should've swapped roles because I was fucking diabolical in that film – I should've got nicked for impersonating an actor. Anyway, I digress . . . a big word for me – seven letters.

So there's a bit of a buzz going on with a few people running about on deck, and all of a sudden we're summoned downstairs to this big room with a telly in it. This is the whole fucking crew by the way, with me and Donald hiding at the back like two naughty schoolboys. Then somebody announces it's the 'Most Beautiful Man in the World' Awards.

Well, obviously me and the Don think we might be in the running here, but hold up, the next announcement tells us that our very own Matthew McConaughey is one of the nominees and he's up against that other alright-looking geezer, George Clooney. Anyway, the show begins and Matthew is giving it the old 'Woo! Woo!' like the Yanks do when they get excited. After about five minutes of this bollocks I wanna be somewhere else – anywhere else. Yeah, I suppose I might be a little bit jealous. I mean, he ain't a bad-looking fella . . .

As they're building up to the big moment the television shows this satellite going across the world from east to west. Funny how everything and everyone seems to travel from east to west. Maybe they're following the sun – wanting to find out where it goes before it comes up the other side again – or maybe they thought it went down a hole. Anyway, this satellite is travelling across Europe and as it's getting closer to London, I'm thinking, 'You never know . . .'

Bang! It hits London and with all the lapping up that's going on I can't contain myself any more. I shout out, 'Stop right there, my son! That's me!' The Aussies, who have a great sense of humour – well, they're cockney Irish, ain't they? Or at least the majority are – are all giggling. But as far as the others are concerned, it goes straight over their heads.

Eventually the satellite gets to America and we're into Clooney and McConaughey territory. We creep quietly past George and slip loudly into Texas, and at this point it's announced that Matthew is the winner. He goes absolutely potty – like he's scored the winning goal in the World Cup final and won the Heavyweight Championship of the World in one go.

I'm thinking, 'Fuck me, what a prat!'

The whole thing just seems a bit embarrassing, but then on re-flection I start to think maybe this is the big difference between us – apart from my good looks, of course. Maybe this is what makes Matthew a film star, which he is – at the time of writing he's just won an Oscar, and deservedly so.

Anyway, once I finally get back up on deck, the whole thing kinda makes me think about where I've come from. Looking at Australia, 14,000 miles away from home – literally on the other side of the world – I start thinking about me and my mate Tony Yeates as kids in the East End, and I start thinking about Captain Cook. There's a plaque on the Mile End Road which marks the start of his journey to Oz. It's just opposite the place a club called Nashville's used to be, where me and Tony had a few adventures of our own in the late seventies. We'd often find ourselves gazing unsteadily up at that plaque after we'd had a few on a Friday night – dreaming of travelling the world, the places we might see and the people we might meet. And suddenly standing on that ship in the southern hemisphere, it comes to me: 'I've made that journey. I've done what Cook did!'

Alright, he did it on a sailing ship and I did it First Class British Airways, but I've done it just the same. I'm not trying to book myself as being on Cook's level as an explorer, but for someone who comes from where I do, getting to the Great Barrier Reef was still some kind of achievement. That was when the idea of paying my own tribute to the places and the people that made me what I am (I won't be demanding actual blue plaques: 'Ray Winstone narrowly escaped a good kicking here' etc.) started to make me smile. I hope it will do the same for you.

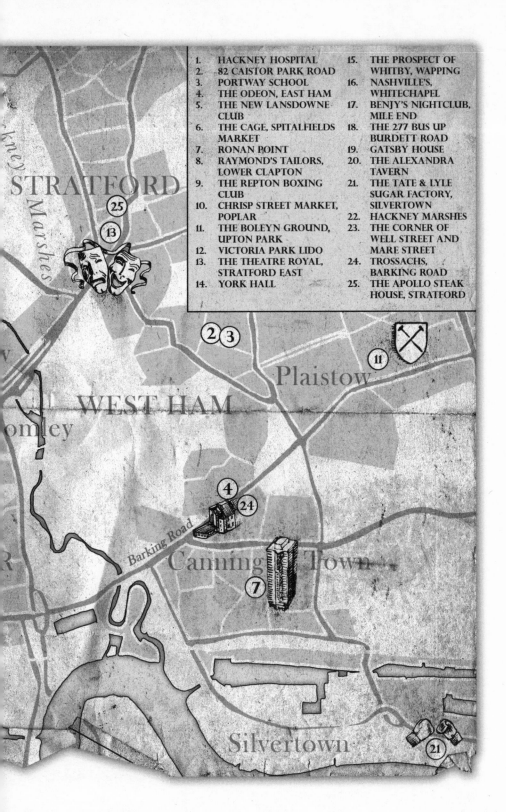

1. HACKNEY HOSPITAL
2. 82 CAISTOR PARK ROAD
3. PORTWAY SCHOOL
4. THE ODEON, EAST HAM
5. THE NEW LANSDOWNE CLUB
6. THE CAGE, SPITALFIELDS MARKET
7. RONAN POINT
8. RAYMOND'S TAILORS, LOWER CLAPTON
9. THE REPTON BOXING CLUB
10. CHRISP STREET MARKET, POPLAR
11. THE BOLEYN GROUND, UPTON PARK
12. VICTORIA PARK LIDO
13. THE THEATRE ROYAL, STRATFORD EAST
14. YORK HALL
15. THE PROSPECT OF WHITBY, WAPPING
16. NASHVILLE'S, WHITECHAPEL
17. BENJY'S NIGHTCLUB, MILE END
18. THE 277 BUS UP BURDETT ROAD
19. GATSBY HOUSE
20. THE ALEXANDRA TAVERN
21. THE TATE & LYLE SUGAR FACTORY, SILVERTOWN
22. HACKNEY MARSHES
23. THE CORNER OF WELL STREET AND MARE STREET
24. TROSSACHS, BARKING ROAD
25. THE APOLLO STEAK HOUSE, STRATFORD

CHAPTER 1

HACKNEY HOSPITAL

When I look back through the history of my family, we've done fuck all for this country. I don't mean that in a bad way. The Winstones weren't villains. We've always been grafters, back and forthing between the workhouse and the public house. But at the time I was born – in Hackney Hospital on 19 February 1957 – the Second World War was still very much on people's minds. It's probably a bit of a cliché to say 'everyone had lost somebody', but in our family, it wasn't even true. Maybe it was more the luck of the draw in terms of their ages than anything else, but there was no one you could put your finger on and say they had sacrificed themselves in any way.

Doodlebugs rained down on Hackney – I remember being told about one going straight up Well Street – but none of them hit my nan and granddad's flat in Shore Place. They had to go in the air-raid shelter round the front a few times, but their three young sons – my dad Ray and his two brothers, Charlie and Kenny – were safely evacuated out towards High Wycombe. The village they were lodged in lost three men on HMS *Hood*, so that was about as close as the war got to them.

Uncle Kenny, my dad's younger brother, got a start as a jockey and rode a few winners for Sir Gordon Richards' stable. I've always surmised that he must've picked up his way with horses when he was evacuated to the countryside, because there weren't too many racecourse gallops in the East End. That said, his dad, my granddad, Charles Thomas Winstone, did work as a tic-tac man, passing on the odds for bookmakers at tracks all around Britain, so horse-racing was kind of in Kenny's blood.

When he got too tall to be a jockey on the flat any more, Kenny became a butcher. I guess that was one way he could carry on working with animals. He ended up with a couple of shops – one in Well Street, and one just round the back of Victoria Park – so he did alright. But before that he'd been a pretty good boxer as well. He boxed for the stable boys, and once fought at the Amateur Boxing Association (ABA) finals against a mate of my dad's called Terry Spinks, who went on to win a gold medal at the Melbourne Olympics aged only eighteen, and would later be known for raising the alarm as the Black September terrorists approached the Israeli athletes' quarters when he was coaching the South Korean team at the Munich Olympics in 1972. Apparently he gave old Spinksy a bit of a fright.

This wouldn't have come as any great surprise in the Winstone household, because boxing was what the men in our family did. My granddad had been drafted into a Scottish regiment and stationed in Edinburgh for a while just to be on their boxing team, and when my dad did his National Service with the Royal Artillery, he spent virtually the whole three years in his tracksuit, boxing out of Shoeburyness. I think Henry Cooper might've been doing his stint at around the same time, and the only actual service I ever remember my dad telling me about was helping out after the great flood of 1953, when all those people died on Canvey Island.

He said he'd got really angry because the Salvation Army wouldn't give him a cup of tea when he didn't have the money to buy one. From then on if he ever saw someone selling *The War Cry*, he'd just tell 'em to go away. He had no time for those people whatsoever, to the extent that I even remember asking him about it once as a kid: 'Surely there must be some good people in the Salvation Army, Dad?' But he just told me, 'Nah, son, they wouldn't give me a cup of tea.'

Hopefully this has given you a bit of an introduction to the kind of men I grew up around. I'm going to have to go back a bit further in time for the women, because I came across a story recently which really answered a lot of questions for me about the way I think, and the way the women in my family live their lives. It all started when the Winstones got turned down by the BBC TV series *Who Do You Think You Are?*

Now, I like that programme – I get right into it (although I have seen some boring ones) – but the first time they asked, I didn't really want to do it. I enjoy watching them go through other people's ancestors' dirty laundry, but when it came to mine, I just didn't really want to know. That's all in the past, and it's the future you want to be thinking about. They kept coming back to me, though, and in the end I thought, 'Do you know what? Maybe it would be good to find out a few things.'

I knew I had a great-uncle Frank – my granddad's brother on my mum's side – who played centre-forward for West Ham. He was at Reading first, and then he moved to West Ham in 1923, the year they got to their first Wembley final. Maybe if they'd bought him before the big game instead of just after it, they might actually have won. As it happens, they got beat, and my great-uncle Frank was a kind of consolation prize, but still, I thought that might be a good starting point.

Unfortunately, it seems that on the show they stick to the direct bloodline, i.e. parents and children only, so an uncle can't be the story, or at least that's what they told me. And after giving due consideration to the mountain of material that their researchers had unearthed, they had come to the conclusion that the various roots and branches of the Winstone family tree were just too fucking boring to make a show out of. They were lovely about it – 'Sorry, Ray, but there's nothing in here we can use' – and I did get the giggles on the phone. That can't have been an easy call to make: 'Listen, Fatboy, there's just nothing interesting about you or your family.'

It's funny looking back, but I was quite depressed about it for a while – not depressed so I wanted to kill myself, just a bit disappointed and choked up. But then I sat down and went through some of the stuff they'd dug up, and I actually got really enlightened by it.

The one thing that did come out of *Who Do You Think You Are?* was that both branches of my family had been East Londoners for as far back as they could trace. Right the way back to the 1700s my mum's side came from Manor Park/East Ham and my dad's from Hoxton and the borders of the City.

OK, my family never changed the world. They never invented penicillin or found the Northwest Passage or won a VC at the Siege of Mafeking. They were basically just people who sometimes fell on hard times and ended up in the poorhouse for a couple of weeks – or longer. But there was one extraordinary thing about them, as there is about any family that's still around today, and this was that they survived. On top of that, it turned out we did have one story worth telling after all, because some time afterwards the same TV company came back to me and said they were making another show that they did want me to be a part of. The subject? There's a thick ear for anyone who's guessed it: asylums.

The researchers had discovered that my great-great-grandmother (on my dad's side) was originally married to a Merchant Navy man called James Stratton, who ended up in the old Colney Hatch Lunatic Asylum at Friern Barnet. That was somewhere I'd end up too a century and a bit later, albeit for slightly different reasons – I was shooting the movie version of *Scum* – but poor old seaman Stratton had got syphilis.

I didn't find out until we were researching the programme – they like the historians and other experts to break the news to you as you're going along, so they can catch you looking surprised – just how rife syphilis was in Victorian London. Even before that, going back to Hogarth's time in the eighteenth century, all those wigs they were wearing in his paintings weren't just fashion accessories, they were there to cover the fucking scars.

One strange thing that happened was that at one point it actually became fashionable to be syphilitic, so people would wear false noses and ears to make it look like they had it when they didn't. Wearing a false nose to show you were a proper geezer – how nutty was that? No crazier than covering yourself in tattoos or having plastic surgery you don't medically need, I suppose.

As far as the unfortunate Mr Stratton was concerned, they thought he'd probably picked the syphilis up in the Navy, before he was married, but then he might have had a dabble again, because the sixth of his eight children was born with it too. Either way, he died a terrible death, leaving my great-great-grandmother alone with all those kids, and no real means of support – visible or invisible.

At this point in the story, the odds must've been on her drifting into prostitution. That's certainly what I thought was going to happen. Because all these events were unfolding around Whitechapel, and the name she went by at the time, Hannah Stratton, had a familiar ring to it – like Mary Kelly or one of those other tragic victims – in my head we were heading towards Jack the Ripper territory. Obviously the programme-makers don't tell you what's going to happen because they want you to cry. In fact, they want that so badly they're practically standing behind the camera with a big bowl of freshly chopped onions.

They'd taken me to Christ Church, Spitalfields, the big white church opposite the market my dad used to take me to as a kid when he was in the fruit and veg game. I didn't remember ever having been inside before – me and my family not being churchy kind of people, and in any case it was boarded up and virtually derelict for most of the sixties and seventies – but it looks amazing now it's all been restored. So I'm standing there in this beautiful place, waiting for the bad news about Hannah getting gruesomely done in by the Ripper, and then they tell me that it was in this church that she married her second husband.

It turned out that Stratton wasn't actually my great-great-grandfather at all, because Hannah managed to marry again within a year of his death. She would probably have been ostracised at first because of the syphilis, and could easily have headed for the nearest gin palace and ended up in the gutter somewhere, but instead she thought, 'Fuck it, I'm fighting for my kids.' So she stood her ground and her neighbours rallied round to help her – which was incredible in itself, because that kind of thing doesn't happen so much today, at least not in cities, where no one tends to know who the people living next door to them are any more.

After Hannah remarried and became Mrs Durham, she and her new husband lived round the corner from Christ Church – for a while, and then moved to West Hackney. Her syphilis became dormant and she had more kids, so that was when my granddad's father was born. Her second husband had only been twenty-seven when they married – effectively a toyboy, and she never marked his card about exactly how old she was. So, while he thought she eventually died at the ripe old age of sixty-one, it was probably a good bit riper than that.

You couldn't blame her for dangling the carrot a bit, though, given that she had kids to look after. And if she hadn't done it, I wouldn't be here today, so it was a happy ending for me as well. (And for the programme-makers, because Hannah's story did make me cry. It broke my heart, to be honest, but it also made me very proud of her, and glad I'd done the show as now I can pass the story on down through my family to make sure she's not forgotten.)

All in all, Hannah Durham was an amazing old girl, and I could see a lot of the characteristics of my sister Laura and my auntie Irene, my dad's sister, in her. Not that either of them have ever had syphilis, but I've got a lot of strong women in my family. Obviously my mum's is a different line, but it's the same on her side as well. We'll get to my maternal grandma and her three husbands in the next chapter . . .

In the meantime, the long and the short of it is that the men in my family seem to like marrying strong women, probably because we need them to keep us in line. But the other thing I realised standing in that old Hawksmoor church – and I know this might sound overly romantic, a bit pony even – was the depth of my family's connection to the area.

My dad was born in Hoxton. You could definitely hear the bells of St Mary-le-Bow on Cheapside from there, so that makes him a proper cockney. And as I've said, the family had been basically there or thereabouts since the 1700s, until his generation started to move away in the late sixties. Yet now, just a few decades later, I've got cousins in Dunmow, Braintree, Watford, Bushey, but there's none of us left inside the M25: we've all got let out for good behaviour. How and why that change came about, and what it meant to us and to others, is one of the main subjects of this book.

I still think of myself as an East Londoner rather than a Londoner. And as I was driving in to do that filming in Spitalfields from where I live now, out in Essex, I seemed to pass places that had some relevance to mine or my family's lives every few hundred yards from Whipps Cross onwards. None of the actual people are there any more, but that doesn't make the memories any less vivid. It might even bring them through more strongly – after all, you don't need to remember things that are still happening.

We were a big old tribe, and when I was a kid we used to have a big get-together more or less every Sunday, but now we're much more dispersed, and the unit has kind of contracted much more to immediate family. My cousins all keep in touch, but I've been guilty of letting that go a bit in recent years. The way people perceive you is part of it as well. You start living in a bigger house and they'll tell you, 'Oh, we went past yours the other day', so you'll say, 'Well, why didn't you fucking knock on the door?' But if the door's behind a security gate, then the fact that they don't knock on it is as much your fault as anyone else's, isn't it?

Looking back now, I can clearly see the staging posts by which the old closeness started to leave us. When my mum and dad brought me back from Hackney Hospital in the winter of 1957 (the building's still there, up on Homerton High Street – I think it was the tall Victorian-looking wing to the east, not the lower section where the entrance is – but last time I looked they'd turned it into a nuthouse in my honour), they didn't have a home of their own yet. From what I've gathered, there was never any question but that the three of us would stay in the flat in Shore Place with my dad's parents for a little while after my birth.

At a time when families would generally stay in the same place, nans and granddads were the nucleus of everything – everyone else would circulate around them. Now they just tend to get left where they are when everyone moves away, and then you see 'em when you can. It's no wonder they get a bit grumpy. I feel lucky to have grown up at the tail-end of the old way of doing things, because the world of my childhood could not have wished for a better focus than my granddad Charles – Toffy they called him, I suppose because he was a bit of a toff – and Nanny Maud.

He was a real one-off, my grandfather; an old-fashioned gentleman. I'm sure a lot of people say that about their grandparents, but in this case it was definitely true. Toffy was a short, wiry man who always dressed immaculately and never forgot to lift his hat to the ladies as he walked down the road. By all accounts – at least, all accounts of his own – he was the man behind the modernisation of tic-tacking (the complex sign language for communicating bookmakers' odds which you used to see John McCririck doing on the telly, until Channel 4 Racing gave him the Spanish – as in Spanish Archer, the El Bow). I think he definitely simplified it, him and another fella . . . there's always another fella.

Nanny Maud was a similarly upright individual. I think she'd run a café as a younger woman, but by the time I came along everyone called her 'The Schoolteacher', because she had a lovely proper way of talking. She wasn't all gorblimey, she was much more 'telephone voice'. Even nowadays, when you meet the really old East London boys and girls, I find they have that almost Dickensian style of speaking which is nothing like how I sound. There's still an accent, but it's all very clipped and correct, and it's a beautiful thing to hear.

I don't have any specific recollections of sharing a home with Toffy and Maud as a child, because we moved out of there when I was about a year old. But some of my happiest early childhood memories are of the days when Maud would take me to the toy shop in Mile End – just by the junction where they've put that silly grass roof over the main road – and buy me Airfix kits, or the Batmobile with a Bat-boat that fired little rockets out the back. And in my teens I'd actually end up living with my granddad for a year, which would turn out to be one of the most influential, as well as the funniest, times in my life.

Hospitals take away as well as giving, and in my early teens Nanny Maud would die in the same place I'd been born. She had a fall and never quite got over it, and I don't think the family could ever forgive Hackney Hospital for the feeling that a bit more could've been done. I was a kid on the cusp of being a young man by that stage, and I remember the sombre, grown-up mood of the family gathering in the Jackdaw & Stump – the pub just along the high street from the hospital – when everyone had come up to visit Nan together after her fall.

We were all worried about her, and at times like that you obviously feel an atmosphere of foreboding in the air, but I don't think any of us realised how big a change was coming. People often think of the granddad as being the head of a family, but I think it's the nan, really. Obviously once she's gone, you still go and see him – and Toffy did a pretty good job of managing by himself, he even got himself a nice girlfriend after a while – but you can see how lost the men in the family are once the maternal mainstay is gone. From then on, there's less and less reason for everyone to get together, and the whole family starts to break up.

It was probably a good job I didn't know all that on the day of her funeral, because I was upset enough already. This was the first loss

I was old enough to really feel properly. I remember being outside the flats where all the flowers were laid out ready to be taken to the cemetery, when I heard some local kid ask 'Who's dead?' quite rudely and I lost the plot. I couldn't cope with that at all – it seemed very disrespectful – and things went pear-shaped for a few seconds, before I was told in no uncertain terms to keep quiet and have a little bit of dignity about myself.

'Who's dead?' is never the right question to ask, though, is it? If someone says, 'Who's passed?' you can tell they're making an effort, but 'Who's dead?' is just too brutal. That's not to say there's no room for levity when someone's died. Quite the reverse. I remember it used to be a big event for my dad and his mates – and we still do it today – when someone would say, 'There's a bit of underground sports on Thursday.' What that means is there's a funeral, and a funeral means a wake, which means a blinding party.

The funny thing about 'underground sports' is, it's OK for us to talk about them, but we'd still reserve the right to take it amiss if someone else did it at the wrong moment. I love that kind of hypocritical cockney morality. That is very much the tradition I was brought up in, like with the old boys off the docks, they'd be telling you some great stories and effing and blinding all the way through (the expression 'swear like a docker' doesn't come from nowhere), but heaven help you if you swore in front of their wife on the bus: ''Scuse me . . . 'scuse me . . . oi! 'Scuse me! Not in front of the wife.' I do understand and respect that way of doing things – it's kind of my way of doing things too, if I'm honest – but it does have its flaws.

CHAPTER 2

CAISTOR PARK
ROAD, PLAISTOW

When I started writing this book the first thing I did was go back to the street I lived on as a kid. I wanted to have a look around to see if people or incidents I'd forgotten would come flooding back to me. What I couldn't get over was how much smaller everything was than the way I remembered it. Obviously when you're little you're down at hedge and gate level, so the world looks massive to you, but there was more to it than that. Going back to Plaistow now, it feels very quiet and suburban, whereas in my childhood there seemed to be people everywhere, and something was always happening.

Of course at that time – in the late fifties – the London docks were still working at full speed and strength. The southern end of our road wasn't far away from the Royal Victoria and Royal Albert Docks, so a lot of the hustle and bustle of the neighbourhood (not to mention the odd bit of unofficial bounty from shipping crates that had accidentally on purpose fallen open in transit) could be traced back to there.

The docks are long gone now, or at least the idea that anyone would use them for unloading stuff from boats is. But my home from the age of one to the age of eight – 82 Caistor Park Road, Plaistow – is still very much there, looking more or less unchanged over the intervening half century.

It's a boxy, two-storey house near the end of a terrace. When we first moved in, we lived upstairs while an old lady and her sister kept the ground floor. Then after my sister Laura came along – in February 1959 – the Winstones took over the downstairs as well. There was never a bathroom (I'm assuming they've got one now). We had an outside toilet in the small back garden, and a tin bath would come out in the front room when it was time for a scrub-up.

In my early years my mum had to keep me on reins, because as soon as I saw daylight, I'd be off like a greyhound out of the trap (my eldest girl Lois was the same). But from pretty much the moment Laura and I were old enough to walk around unaided, we played outside in the street all day. There were very few cars about in those times, and we still had a milkman with a horse-drawn cart. He'd come round the corner at a set time every morning, and since all the kids knew he was coming we'd have plenty of time to put bricks in the middle of the road so he'd have to go round them like he was doing a slalom, shouting, 'You little bastards!' as he went.

At the north end of Caistor Park Road was, and is, the main drag down to Stratford, and beyond that thoroughfare stretches the wide open space of West Ham Park, which is still a lovely bit of grass to have a walk around. Returning to the area now, I can see that the houses at the top of the road tend to be much better finished off, whereas our bit is more of a khazi. Don't go down my end – it's a shithole.

I don't recall it being that way when I was a kid, but then again, in my memories the sun has always got his hat on. Even though my rational mind knows Londoners were still afflicted by deadly pea-souper fogs at that time, all I can remember is clear skies and long days of unbroken sunshine.

In my mind, Plaistow in the early sixties is like one of those adverts filmed in New York where it's a hot day and someone knocks the top of the fire hydrant off, except done the English way – with a hosepipe. Over the years you do colour your memories in a bit (at least, I have done), but I'm going to try and keep them as toned down and close to reality as possible. Obviously you're only going to be seeing things from my point of view, because that's what an autobiography is all about. But I realise there's at least one other side to a lot of these stories – just ask Matthew McConaughey – and if someone's given me another perspective, I'm not going to hold back on it.

For instance, I look back on myself as a little boy and I think I was alright, but my aunties always tell me I was a right little fucker. I'll insist I was a nice kid and they'll say, 'No, you were an absolute fucker – always up to something.'

Now that must be true, because it's not the sort of thing they're gonna make up, so I have to start thinking about how they might've got that idea. I do remember there was a little parade of shops round the corner from our house where I used to sing for the greengrocer and he would give me a banana – well, every showbiz career has got to start somewhere, hasn't it? I was still in the pram, so I couldn't have been that old, but one day I sang for him and he didn't give me one and I told him to fuck off. My mum would laugh telling me that story years later, but she was embarrassed at the time because she very rarely swore, so wherever I'd picked that word up from, it hadn't been from her. And 'No, you'll have no banana' was my first bad review. There've been a few more since . . .

In Plaistow in the fifties and sixties, there used to be a shop on every corner, and the one change to my immediate childhood surroundings which I really couldn't get my head round when I went back on my fact-finding mission was that the old corner shop is now just a normal house. The shopkeeper's name was Mr Custard, which was obviously a gift to us as kids. He had a big shock of unruly white hair and looked a bit like Mr Pastry. We used to terrorise him, going in there and shouting 'Cowardy, cowardy Custard, can't eat mustard!' You know what kids are like. I feel quite sorry for him now, as he was probably a nice old boy.

A lot of good people lived on Caistor Park Road. A couple of doors up from us was a girl called Sylvie who lived with her mum – I don't remember a dad, and there might not have been one. She must have been in her mid-teens and she used to babysit for us and take me up the park. One day, before my sister was born, she was pushing me to the swings in my stroller when a geezer jumped out in front of us and flashed her. I was only a baby, so I don't seem to have accrued any deep psychological scars, but when my parents told me the story they were still really impressed that she hadn't just fucked off and left me. She was a lovely girl, Sylvie, and it was very sad that a few years later she committed suicide. I always hoped it wasn't what happened in the park that day that upset her.

Everyone living on Caistor Park Road knew everyone else, and all the stuff you always hear about windows being left open and it being OK to leave a key hanging behind the door was still true. There was even an old girl living on her own over the way who my mum used to cook dinner for. She had no connection with our family, other than that she lived near us. I know this sounds corny, but people looked after people. They really did. Every time you went out of the house in the morning you'd see women doing their steps and their windows. I know that sounds a bit chauvinistic now, but how can it be a bad thing for people to have taken pride in themselves and in their community?

Our home was always spotless, inside and out. My mum made sure everything was in its place and everything was done properly. She'd learnt that from her mother, who was not a woman to be trifled with.

My nan on my mum's side was called Dolly Richardson, but she was always Nanny Rich to me. We called her Nanny Rich because she was . . . rich. By the time I was born, she owned a fair bit of property in the Plaistow, Manor Park and Forest Gate areas, and I think it was down to her that we ended up living where we did. She was a furrier by trade – not a farrier shoeing horses, a furrier making coats – and she'd done well enough to move out of East London to Shoeburyness, just along the Essex Riviera from Southend, after the war. There are a few fur coats left in the family somewhere, but obviously you can't wear 'em any more because someone will throw paint over you. I presume there must have been a few quid poking around when Nanny Rich – God rest her soul – eventually went away in the early eighties, but I never saw any of it.

Nanny Rich was married three times – once more than old Hannah Durham – and she outlived all of her husbands. We'd started to look at her in a different way by the end. Her short-lived first husband, my auntie Olive's father, wasn't my grandfather. That was Husband Number Two. My mum's dad was Mr Richardson (no relation to the notorious South London clan), but he died before I was old enough to really get to know him. By all accounts he was a very tall man, and the only one in the family who ever fought in the First World War. True to form for my family he came out of it in one piece, but it's possible his death in the late fifties may have been caused by the lingering effects of mustard gas forty years before. I remember being in bed one night and hearing my mum distressed and crying, but not really knowing why he'd died or what that meant.

My nan's last husband, Reg Hallett, who she married after a decent interval, was a terrific old boy. I had a lot of time for him. Reg was a mason – a very well-to-do man from Shoeburyness, which sounds like an Ian Dury song. I think he worked in Churchill's Treasury during the war. When I got a bit older he used to beg me to become a mason too, but I wasn't having it.

Whoever she ended up marrying, mason or otherwise, Nanny Rich never stopped being her own boss. I believe she made fur coats for the Royal Family, although that is the sort of thing that sometimes gets said without too much evidence to back it up. She definitely made them for Donald Campbell, though – the Bluebird man who held the land and water speed records simultaneously and died in that terrible crash on Coniston Water – which is no less impressive in a way, as Campbell was renowned for enjoying the good things in life, and no doubt knew a nice bit of fur when he saw it.

This is probably as good a moment as any to tell the story of my childhood brush with another snappy dresser: Ronnie Kray. I think how my dad knew the twins was that when they were kids they'd all boxed at the New Lansdowne, a club on Mare Street in Hackney which my granddad Toffy was on the board of. Reg and Ron were actually pretty good boxers before other more nefarious activities began to take precedence.

I was still a baby the day Ronnie Kray came round to Caistor Park Road to see my dad, but I've been told this story so many times that I can see it unfolding in my head. Obviously everyone's on their best behaviour, but then Ronnie picks me up, and by all accounts I've pissed all over him. He's got a new Mac on, which has probably cost a few bob, and I've absolutely covered it. Everyone's laughing. Well, not at first. At first they're all thinking, 'Fucking hell, he's pissed on

Ronnie Kray!' But then Ronnie cracks up, so everyone else knows it's safe to join in.

Cups of tea get drunk, and him and my dad have a talk about whatever it is they need to talk about, and then everyone breathes a sigh of relief when Ronnie leaves. The Kray brothers hadn't yet reached the peak of their notoriety by that time, but people still knew who they were. The funny thing was that earlier on the same day my dad had got in a row with a bloke who lived up the road, and after Ronnie fucked off to get his coat dry-cleaned, this guy came round going, 'Look, we've only had an argument – there's no need to bring them into it.' Obviously there was no way my dad would ever have done that. If he needed to have a fight with a bloke up the road, he was quite capable of doing that on his own initiative, without calling in the Krays for back-up.

Readers are entitled to a measure of curiosity about what mutually advantageous business Ron and Ray might have been discussing. There was a time while I was still very young when my dad was possibly up to all sorts, with or without Ron and Reg, but I think something happened that he didn't like when he was out with them in Walthamstow once. He only told me this years later – and even then in quite a cryptic, Edwardian kind of way – but I think my dad saw someone get stabbed, fairly brutally, and he just thought it was unnecessary. When is that kind of violence ever anything else? But for my dad I think that was the moment he thought, 'Not only is this wrong, but also it ain't for me.'

He wasn't going to be joining the Salvation Army any time soon, but from the time I was old enough to remember, he was mostly working on the markets. Not only my dad's two brothers but also most of his friends seemed to work in either the meat market, the fish market or the fruit market, so we never went hungry. My dad started off on the meat at Smithfield Market, but then moved to fruit and veg. Either he got caught nicking something, or they were trying to guarantee the family a balanced diet (given that his brother Kenny already had a butcher's).

There was a fair bit of ducking and diving going on in those days. It still wasn't long since the end of the war, and people needed a bit of a lift – especially as even though we'd won, we seemed to be re-building places like Berlin and Munich (which had admittedly been smashed to pieces) before we got started on our own cities. At that time people reckoned that the best job was the bread round, because you'd get your wage and pay your little bit of tax – whatever that was at the time – but you'd also have your own bread. That was your bunce. It was allowed. The company knew it went on but turned a blind eye, and the bread-man lived a good life.

It was the same on the docks, where a few of my dad's friends who didn't work on the markets seemed to earn a crust. There they even had a name for it: 'spillage'. A box would get dropped, and whatever the contents were, the people working there were allowed to keep. I suppose that kind of thing would be looked upon as theft today, but I prefer to think of it as 'garnish' – that little something extra which meant we didn't go hungry and always had a shirt on our back and shoes on our feet.

My dad's eldest brother Charlie was doing a little bit better than that. He'd got a job in the print when he was younger. Those jobs were so well paid that what they used to do was sub them out – some geezer would give you half his wage if you let him take over from you, and that gave you money to go and do something else. Charlie went on to own his own factory which upholstered settees. He was very generous and would always give us a ten-bob note every time we saw him. He usually had nice cars as well – often those big old

Rovers that look like Bristols – and he'd let my dad borrow them sometimes if we were going somewhere nice.

I think Maud and Toffy might've lost as many as three kids (ages ranging from infant to young child, and at least one of them to whooping cough, which was rife at the time) to leave them with just the three boys and my auntie Irene. That was the main reason people had bigger families in those days – to cover themselves, because you were probably going to lose a few.

Laura and I had plenty of other 'uncles' who weren't genetically our uncles to make up the numbers. A lot of them worked in the fish market at Billingsgate, like Frankie Tovey, who was a Catholic, and Ronnie Jacobs, who was Jewish. We were Church of England, but people's religious denomination was something you only tended to find out about later in life. Like with my best mate Tony Yeates: even though we basically grew up together from my mid-teens onwards, I only found out he was a Catholic when he got married. No one ever knew, and I think London's always been a bit like that. It's one of the great things about it in a way. Basically, who gives a fuck?

It was the same with my dad's mate Lenny Appleton – 'Apples' everyone called him – who was gay. He was a terrific guy, always immaculately turned out, and all the girls loved him, but no one ever worried about who he was having sex with. I'm talking about a load of hairy-arsed geezers here who didn't give a fuck for anyone. They were the chaps – out pulling birds and doing what they were doing – and what Lenny got up to on his own time just wasn't a problem for them. When someone's your mate, they're your mate, and that's all there is to it.

I found out some interesting things about the situation with homosexuality in old London – and sexuality in general – when I was making that TV show about Hannah Durham. It turned out that people in those times were much less prudish than we tend to think of them as being, and than we are now. It was only towards the end of the Victorian era that everyone started to get more buttoned up.

In terms of public life, everything was still pretty much under wraps by the fifties, but looking back at the way Apples was accepted by my dad and his mates, it gives you a fresh perspective on people who weren't necessarily highly educated. They weren't moving in the supposedly enlightened circles of the art or literary worlds. These were geezers who worked in markets and had their own street education and would often be presented as quite brutal – shouting 'Fucking poof' at Quentin Crisp in TV dramas or whatever – so it's quite refreshing to realise that they weren't always like that. In fact, it was a shame the people who actually had power in the country weren't as tolerant as my dad and his mates. People who come from where I come from don't get to make the laws, we just get to break them.

There was a tradition on my dad's side of our family of naming eldest sons after their father, so my uncle Charlie's son got called Charlie-boy. My dad – as those of you who are on the ball will already have noticed – was Ray, so a lot of my relatives used to (and still do sometimes) call me 'Ray-Ray' to differentiate between us. When I got a bit older, my dad's mates also used to know me as 'Little Sugs', because his nickname was 'Sugar', in honour of the great Sugar Ray Robinson.

There were signs from very early on that I was going to carry on the family's pugilistic tradition. The nursery school I went to was up on the main road on the way to Stratford. I got suspended from it once for having a fight with another kid on a climbing frame. It was only a skirmish, and I don't think I was a generally disruptive presence, although you probably won't be surprised to hear that this was not to be the last educational establishment I would be suspended or expelled from.

I loved that place, though. They used to get us all to lie down and have a kip in the afternoon, and you didn't just get free milk in a little bottle, you got orange juice as well. The only other thing I remember really clearly was that every kid was allocated their own special decorated peg for putting your coat on, and mine was a camel – probably because I always had the hump.

CHAPTER 3

PORTWAY SCHOOL

Our house was a happy house, and it was also a loud house – in good times and in bad. Sometimes there'd be rows, and sometimes there'd be parties, but Sunday mornings were always the same. Dad would go out and get the bagels, and then Laura and I would get into his and mum's bed while she did the breakfast. We had a little pink-and-white Pye record player, and we'd listen to some Frank Sinatra, Jack Jones or Judy Garland on it while Dad read the papers. Then after breakfast we'd get smartened up in our best clothes and head over to Hackney to see the grandparents.

At other times, the family would come to us. When we were in Plaistow, we always used to have a big party on Bonfire Night. My dad's brothers and sister would come round with their kids and we'd make a load of noise in the garden. All the fireworks would be kept in the outside toilet to keep them dry and warm. One time, Uncle Charlie went in there for a more traditional purpose and a Jumping Jack went under the door. We heard a kerfuffle inside and everyone was laughing, then out came Uncle Charlie swearing and running round the garden. The Jumping Jack was in his trousers. He was lucky he'd come out the door because you wouldn't want that blowing up in a confined space.

Another evening – I want to think of it as the same night but it would almost certainly have been a different one – the party was in full flow when a policeman turned up, on a motorbike, wearing one of the old strap helmets like in *The Blue Lamp*. He knocked on the door and asked for Sugar – all the local coppers knew my dad's nickname, not least because about nine out of ten Old Bill in those days came from the area they policed – then told him there'd been a complaint about the noise. This was unusual so it must've been loud. My dad was very polite about it, and invited the copper in and gave him a drink, and by the end of the night he was giving all the girls rides up and down the street on his motorbike.

They were good times, but it was one law for the law and another for me, as my dad would never let me ride a pushbike, let alone a motorbike. I've been a bit the same with my girls – I'll let them ride a bicycle in the garden, but not outside. (Obviously Lois and Jaime are all grown up now, so I can't stop them going out into the world without stabilisers, but Ellie-Rae is only twelve, so she still has to do things my way.) It wasn't an irrational fear on my dad's part – he'd seen a guy on a bike get his wheel stuck in a tram line on Stratford Broadway once, and the tram had done him.

I remember one tricky moment when my dad came out of the house and saw me riding a mate's bike round the corner. I jumped off it and came charging back up the road, vaulting over everyone's fences to come out behind him on our front path, but I still got a clip round the ear to send me back inside. Those little patches out the front of the houses in Caistor Park Road are nearly all gravelled over now, but in the early sixties there were a lot more postage stamp-sized patches of grass.

Once The Beatles had come along, you'd find us standing between the hedges with our plastic guitars and Beatle wigs on, singing 'She Loves You' and making out we were John, Paul, George or Ringo. Another one of my favourite activities was watching the mods and rockers go roaring down the road like the Lancaster Bombers I used to make Airfix kits of.

All the mods seemed to live on our street, and all the rockers came from the next one down (close enough for me to know how wide of the mark my wardrobe of leathers and Liberace haircut was in *Quadrophenia* fifteen years or so later). They were all mates and they'd all been in the same class at school, but they'd get together to go to Margate or Southend and have a fight on a bank holiday, then for the rest of the year it would all be forgotten.

In terms of historic events which made an impact on people, the one that springs to mind for me is the one that springs to mind for most people, but maybe not for the same reason. Even though I was only six years old at the time, I can clearly remember what I was doing when the news of John F. Kennedy's death broke in November 1963 – I was wondering what all the fuss was about.

Obviously it was sad for him and his family, but I couldn't understand why grown adults were breaking down in tears in the street over something that didn't really have too much to do with them, because he was a Yank. For some reason, everyone seemed to see it as being their business. I suppose because he was young and well liked, and people thought of him as more of a celebrity than a politician.

By then I'd left the afternoon kips and free orange juice of nursery behind for the relatively grown-up world of Portway Primary School. As a kid I never thought of it being 'Portway' as in 'you're on the way to the port' – that's the kind of connection which is lodged so deep in your mind it doesn't really occur to you. And by the time I would've been old enough to get them, those jobs in the docks that might once have been waiting for me had all gone.

You can't be hanging around the gates of your old primary school for too long at my age or people will think you're a nonce. But it made me laugh to retrace the footsteps of my walk to school again all these years later – at the time it felt like miles and miles, but in fact it was only a couple of hundred yards. A little group of us used to assemble on the way down there in the morning, and we'd usually meet up with a mate who had a glass eye. His mum used to let us watch her put it in – you can't believe how much space there is in the socket at the back of the eye – and it used to roll around all over the place until it settled in position.

He'd got his real eye poked out by the spoke of an old bicycle wheel on a bombsite on the main road. With the city to the west and the docks to the south, East London had taken a belting during the Blitz – anything the German bombers had left, they unloaded on us on their way home.

Of course we always won in the endless re-run of the Battle of Britain that was being staged by the Airfix kits hanging from my ceiling, but the fabric of the place I grew up in was definitely holed. If the spaces in the city that the bombsites opened up were the war's legacy to young Londoners, it was our duty to make the most of them. Everyone knew they could be dangerous places which we weren't really meant to hang around in, and that was half the appeal.

A copper caught me messing about in one when I was five or six, and took me straight back to 'Sugar's house', where the punishment for my crime was to be kicked straight upstairs to bed and grounded for a week. It's not just your family, friends and neighbours keeping an eye on you which helps set you on the right road as a kid. If policemen, teachers and doctors know where everyone lives too, that helps you grow up with a sense of being part of a community, rather than just a mass of disconnected individuals. Not that this would stop me getting into a fair amount of mischief, obviously.

Another time when I was messing around on a bombsite I found this big kind of metal torch. I think I'd just watched *Spartacus*, so I knew what to do – I got hold of a box of matches and tried to set fire to some straw in it. Nothing's more interesting to you as a kid than fire, because there's such a big warning sign over it as far as adults are concerned. Unfortunately on this occasion things got a bit more interesting than I'd intended, as some of the flaming straw fell down and set fire to a chair. I was shitting myself after that – every time we walked passed that bombsite I thought the police were after me. And the next few times I went shopping with my mum I'd duck down in the seat of the car if a police car came past, which I suppose was good training for later life.

All the bombsites are gone from Plaistow now, but you can still see where they once were from where the houses stop. A little block of flats in the middle of a terrace is always a tell-tale sign, and where the gaps have been filled in it's like the street has got false teeth.

Not all the memories prompted by seeing my old primary school again are happy ones. Quite early on in my time there I got six of the best across the arse for throwing stones up in the air. OK, one came down and hit another kid on the head, but he wasn't badly hurt, and it was obviously an accident. The headmaster wasn't having any of it though, and he gave me a caning I can still remember to this day. I was absolutely terrified to tell my mum and dad, and the fact that the weals only came to light because my mum was bathing me shows you how young I was.

She asked what had happened so I had to tell her. When my dad found out he went round to the school to hear the headmaster's side of the story. He sat down calmly and listened to his explanation, then when the teacher had finished talking he said, 'So let me get this straight. My boy is five years old, and you've given him six hard wallops across the arse for something he didn't even mean to do?'

I'm not exactly sure what happened next but the impression I got was it was something along the lines of my dad forcing the teacher's head down onto the desk and trying to shove his cane down his throat. Either way, the headmaster never looked at me again, which was a result as far as I was concerned. I did get caned a few times over the years, and sometimes I deserved it, but that one was a fucking liberty.

When you're five or six years old, the boundaries of your world are very clearly defined. Going somewhere in the car was fine, but if I ever walked further than the school, it was like you were Christopher Columbus and didn't know if you were going to fall off the edge of the world.

Apart from Sunday trips over to Hackney to see Maud and Toffy, the main excursion we used to go on would be out of London to see Nanny Rich, Reg Hallett, Auntie Olive and Uncle Len in Shoeburyness. Those drives along the old Southend road seemed to go on forever, and there were three trips which particularly stuck in my mind.

My dad had an old Austin van. If we were all going to squeeze into it, I usually ended up sitting over the engine, between the passenger seat and the driver, which was not so great in the summer. But in the winter I'd be the only one who was warm, especially while the van was lacking a back window, as happened for a while after it got smashed. One time we were driving east in thick snow when the car broke down near the Halfway House pub. Obviously you couldn't just call the AA on your mobile in those days and there wasn't a heater you could put on in the car, so we were absolutely freezing.

I can't actually remember who rescued us on that occasion, but another time we didn't make it all the way to Nanny Rich's house was when we hit a Labrador which ran out in front of us. The dog flew up in the air and came down in the road with a horrible smack, then just got up, shook itself and ran away, apparently none the worse for the impact. We were alright too – just a bit shocked – but my dad's van was not so lucky. The front of it was severely smashed to pieces and there was steam coming out of the radiator, so we had to wait till someone we didn't know stopped to help us. When this guy found out what had happened, he ended up giving me, Mum and Laura a lift all the way back to Plaistow.

That wouldn't happen now – apart from anything else, a woman would be frightened of taking their kids in a car with a stranger – but the geezer genuinely wanted to help and there was a different mentality in those days. I'm not saying there weren't evil fuckers about, because there were, but everyone wasn't so primed by the media always to be thinking about the worst thing that could possibly happen. We didn't have that same fear factor we do now everyone's got Sky News.

In my memory, that change in people's thinking wasn't something that happened gradually. It happened more or less overnight when everyone found out about the Moors Murders. I'm not saying children hadn't been taken away and killed before, but it wasn't something people ever really thought about until Brady and Hindley put it in their heads. In a way, taking away that freedom for parents and children to live without fear was another crime that they committed. Even though it happened all the way up north in the hills outside Manchester, it was such a horrific case and it scared everyone so much that it might as well have happened just up the road. When we got up the next morning after it had been on the news, the streets of East London were empty. A lot of the old freedoms that we used to enjoy had gone out of the window overnight. I must have been eight at the time.

It was a dangerous old road, that one out to Southend. The third – and most dramatic – of the incidents I remember from those drives was the time we drove past a big car crash. There were police everywhere, and as we approached what appeared to be a fair amount of carnage, my mum said, 'Don't look.' Obviously that's the worst thing you can say to a kid – it's right up there with 'Never play with matches'. So by the time we drew level with the scene of the accident, Laura and I both had our faces glued to the window.

I've never forgotten what happened next. Things kind of went into slow motion, as they always seem to at moments of crisis. I suppose it's your body's way of protecting you – the adrenaline speeds up your brain, so whatever else is happening seems to slow down in comparison, which (in theory at least) gives you more time to respond. That's why when we've seen something really horrible, we usually remember every unfolding detail, because it's like we've recorded it so fast that when we try to play it back at normal speed it comes to us in slow motion. Anyway, as we drove past the wrecked car, the back door swung open and a body fell out. I hoped she wasn't dead, but the absent look in that woman's eyes has stayed with me ever since, and there was someone else in the car who looked in a bad way too.

As I'm describing this, I'm realising that it sounds quite like the car-crash sequence in David Lynch's *Wild at Heart*, and probably loads of other films as well. When something shocking's happened to someone and they say it was 'like being in a film', they usually mean it was out of the ordinary. But the reason things happen the way they do on the screen is because a lot of people have got together and done their best to create the illusion of what it actually would be like. So it's no wonder we use those kinds of scenes as a way of understanding reality and distancing ourselves from it at the same time.

I've had similar experiences several times since, of being a witness to really bad things happening. I'm not saying I see dead people like the little boy in *The Sixth Sense* (although I did look a bit like him as a kid), but knowing what death is does change you as a person. And I can understand what they say about people who see a lot of it – whether they be soldiers or doctors, policemen or undertakers – finding that their emotional responses start to close down. We use the word 'deadened' for a reason.

It's the same with me and violence, which I've seen a fair amount of over the years. I've never liked it – and I've liked it less and less as I've grown older – but it doesn't shock me either. I don't see it happen and think, 'Oh, what was that?' I know exactly what it is, and, to a certain extent, I understand it.

CHAPTER 4

THE ODEON,
EAST HAM

When we first arrived there, in the late fifties, Plaistow was in Essex, which used to reach as far into London as Stratford. But from the day they changed all the boundaries around (1 April 1965, and I think we know who the April Fools were – us), the Essex border got pushed back to Ilford, and Plaistow was bundled up with East and West Ham to become part of the Frankenstein London borough of Newham. Why? What did they want to go and do that for?

Essex is one of the great counties of England. You just have to say the name to know what sense it makes: Wessex was to the west and Essex is to the east, with Middlesex somewhere in the middle. But some soppy cunt who sits in a council office somewhere has a bright idea, and all of a sudden something which has worked very well for hundreds of years has got to change, just so he or she can pat themselves on the back for inventing 'Newham'.

Ever since I was a little kid, I've always been really interested in the mythology of East London – the kind of stories which might or might not be true, but which help to define the character of the place either way. One of my mum and dad's best friends was a Merchant Navy man who we called Uncle Tony. I learnt a lot from him – he told me all about his voyages round the world as a young man, which probably helped encourage me to want to travel, as that wasn't something people in my family had tended to do much before. He also had a lot of great stories about the games they used to play in the docks.

For instance, there was one fella whose party piece was to bite the head off a rat. Everyone would bet on whether he could do it or not, then he'd get the rat and put his mouth all around its neck . . . apparently the secret was that you had to do it cleanly, just pull it by the tail and the backbone would come out. Now I'm not recommending anyone try that at home, but being a kid of six or seven and listening to a story like that is certainly going to have an impact on you. As I grew older I loved all the tales about 'spillage' – for some reason, the closer you got to Christmas, crates of whisky would get harder to keep a firm hold of – and the canniness of the docklands characters.

There was one about a geezer who owned a pub that used to do lock-ins for the dockers. They'd stay in there all night and then when it got light the next morning they'd go out and go to work. Obviously he didn't want them to leave, so first he took all the clocks out and then he painted the windows black. They're all in there having a booze up and since it never gets light, he's got them in there forever. Looking at that written down, it seems more like a fairy tale than something which actually happened, but I love the dividing line where something would be on the edge of being made up for the sake of the story.

When I was a bit older and started going to Spitalfields Market with my dad, people used to tell me how all the bollards around Gun

Street and through the old city of London were made from the old cannon that had helped us win the battles of Trafalgar and Waterloo. Now I don't know if that was true or not, but either way it gave me a sense of the history of the place. And if we had any reason to be down in the Shadwell or Wapping areas – where the Ratcliff Highway murders took place more than 200 years ago – I'd usually get told how if you'd gone down there at that time it was like some kind of zoo, because sailors would bring back baby giraffes or lions or monkeys as pets, and by the time they'd get them home they'd be fully grown.

Even as a small boy, I was never averse to a bit of make-believe. I had two little girlfriends called Kim and Tracey who lived just up the road from me. They were twins, and we used to play doctors and nurses together (I think I peaked too soon as a ladies' man). I was always the soldier who came back from the war injured and they had to kiss me better. That was where it all started for me as far as acting was concerned.

Another place that helped incubate the bug was the Odeon, East Ham. There were a couple of local cinemas we used to go to, but this was the main one – it was just near the Boleyn Pub as you go around the West Ham football ground. Do a left onto the Barking road at the end of Green Street and you're there, down by the pie and mash shop (which we never ate at, because my dad hated pie and mash almost as much as he hated the Salvation Army).

It was a beautiful cinema which had opened just before the Second World War with a live show called *Thank Evans* starring Max Miller. You'd go in and the organ would come up from the floor and you'd all have a little sing-song. Then you'd get the B-movie before the main picture – you weren't just in there for a couple of hours, it was the whole afternoon. The first film I ever went to there was *101 Dalmatians*, which came out in 1961, so I must have been four.

My mum took me, and by all accounts I got quite angry with Cruella de Vil, because she was bullying the doggies. Apparently I got out of my seat and ran down the aisle towards the screen waving my fists and shouting 'Cruella de Vil, leave them puppies alone!' I don't actually remember doing this myself – the red mist must've really come down – but Mum told the story so many times I can't forget that it happened.

The slant she put on this incident was that I was so trappy as a kid that I 'even wanted to have a fight with a cartoon'. With hindsight I suppose you could also take it as evidence of how willing I was to get caught up in a drama even then.

Although my mum was the first person who ever took me to the cinema, my dad soon took over the reins. Obviously he had to rise very early to work on the markets. The upside of that was that he tended to be free in the afternoons, and every Wednesday from the age of five onwards he'd pick first me and later me and Laura up from Portway and take us to the pictures. There's a few stories later on that'll show Ray Winstone Senior's harder side, but he was a great dad to us, and I might not be doing what I am now if he'd decided to go down the pub instead of taking his kids to the cinema every week.

Of course, part of his motivation was that he fancied an afternoon kip, but if it was a good film – like *633 Squadron* – he'd stay awake to watch it. I remember him falling asleep in *Jason and the Argonauts*, though, and by the time he'd woken up I'd watched it all the way through twice. We used to see some pretty adult films given how young I was, but the only one I ever remember us being turned away from was a war film called *Hell is for Heroes* with Steve McQueen and James Coburn in it. I think it was an X, which at the time meant sixteen and over, and I remember the ticket-seller (who knew us) very politely telling my dad, 'Sorry, Ray, your boy can't come in.' With hindsight, I can't really fault the guy from the Odeon for that. It is quite a violent film – especially the bit where the guy gets shot and you see his glasses crack – and I was only five years old.

Going to the movies wasn't just a local thing. About once a month, usually on a Sunday afternoon, we'd go up the West End. Cinerama was a big draw then, and we'd go and see big, grown-up films like *Lawrence of Arabia* or *Becket* with O'Toole and Burton – which I loved, even though I was only seven when I first saw it.

My nan and granddad took me to see *How the West was Won* in 70mm, and I had the poster up on my wall with a big map of America and pictures of Annie Oakley on it. Even though grand historical epics were the films I felt most strongly drawn to, I liked stuff that was meant for kids as well. Probably my favourite film of all when I was a youngster was *Mary Poppins*. Where else do you think I got the accent from?

The Sound of Music was good as well – that was definitely one for the West End.

The only small dampener on going to the cinema with the whole family was Laura saying, 'I wanna go toilet.' Sometimes she wouldn't even last till halfway through, and because Mum would have to take her, we'd all have to stand up so they could make their way out into the aisle.

Even though we went up West regularly, sometimes it felt like people there would dig us out a bit. The first time we saw *Zulu* was one of those occasions. It's probably the best film ever, and I know it more or less off by heart now, but the day we went up to Leicester Square to see it has stuck in my mind for a different reason. It's one of the earliest memories I have of people trying to make us feel like we weren't good enough to be somewhere.

We're all sat down, we've got our popcorn, sweets and drinks, and the music's playing. The film hasn't started – I don't think the trailers have even started – and obviously there are a few crackling noises as the bags are opening. But this woman sitting behind us with her Old Man almost barks at us, 'Could you keep the noise down, please?' My mum twists round with a polite half-shrug and explains, 'The film hasn't started yet, darlin' – we're just opening the popcorn and some sweets for the kids.'

Obviously a few more sweet-wrappers get rustled over the next couple of minutes, but no one's making a noise deliberately, and it's still a while before the film's due to start. But the woman can't help herself – she decides to have another go. This time she practically hisses, 'Keep the noise down', and the 'please' is nowhere to be heard. Now my mum's had enough. She stands up, turns round to look the woman straight in the eye and says, 'Do yourself a favour, love, or you'll be wearing it.'

At that point, the pair of them got up and moved. My dad hadn't even said anything – because it was a woman causing the trouble and he would never have a go at a woman. He was probably waiting for the bloke to start and then it would really have gone off. I clearly remember the feeling of 'Oh, sorry, are we not allowed to be here?' Just because we're off our manor, suddenly everyone's going to have something to say about it. This was a feeling I would grow quite familiar with over the years, not just in day-to-day life, but once I started acting as well.

As a small child looking up at that big screen, the idea that I might one day be up there myself would have seemed completely ridiculous. Of course a kid might say they'd 'like to be in a film', in the same way they might want to fly a space rocket or captain England at Wembley, but it wasn't something that was ever going to happen. One of the big differences in those days was you didn't have the Parkinsons or the Wossies – let alone the internet – so film stars were fantasy figures. That was your two hours of escape, and you believed who they were on the screen was who they were in real life.

That said, we did have one film star in the family already. My cousin Maureen, Charlie-boy's sister, was an extra in a Charlie Drake film once. It was set in the Barbican, which was where they lived at that time, and when the film came out we all had to go to the pictures to see Maureen in a big crowd of local kids chasing Charlie Drake down the road at the end. Good luck to anyone trying to get a load of local kids together for a crowd scene in the Barbican these days – you'd have to contact their agents first.

The Odeon East Ham's been through a few changes over the years as well – which one of us hasn't? The last film they showed with the place as an Odeon was Walt Disney's *Sleeping Beauty* in 1981, but then fourteen years later it reopened as the Boleyn Cinema, which was one of the biggest Bollywood cinemas in Britain. They'd have all the dancing films on, and I'd often go past it on the way to and from West Ham games. But when I went back there specially to have a nose around for this book, I saw it had closed down again. Who knows what'll happen next? Maybe someone will buy the place up and re-open it screening Polish art films . . . you never know.

Going back to the Plaistow area in 2014, there's no doubt about what the biggest change is: it's the shift in the ethnic backgrounds of the people who live there. In the space of a couple of generations, it's gone from being the almost entirely white neighbourhood my family moved into, to having the predominantly Asian feel that it undeniably does today. Anyone who thinks a population shift of that magnitude in that short a space of time isn't going to cause a few problems has probably never lived in a place where it's actually happened.

I remember the first black man who came to live on Caistor Park Road. He was a very smart old Jamaican gent who always wore a zoot suit and a hat with a little turn in it. In truth he probably wasn't all that old, he just seemed that way. But he was so novel to us that we just used to stare at him and sometimes even (and I realise this isn't something you'd encourage kids to do today) touch him for luck. He'd just smile and say, 'Hallo, children', in a broad Caribbean accent. He knew we didn't mean any harm by it – we were just kids who hadn't seen a black man before.

I say that, but in fact we had, in the familiar form of Kenny Lynch, who knew my dad. Lynchy had been on the fringes of my dad's world for a while – he was a regimental champion boxer in the Army and went on to have a few hit singles (as well as writing 'Sha La La La Lee' for Newham local heroes the Small Faces) and sing in the kinds of clubs that the Krays used to run – but I'm not sure if he really booked himself as a black man, or wanted anyone else to for that matter.

When the first West Indian and then Asian people moved in, people weren't worried about them; they were a novelty. But as more and more came, a feeling began to develop – particularly with regard to the new arrivals from Bangladesh and Pakistan – that they wanted to just stay in their own community rather than joining in with ours. That was what caused the problems: people sticking with their own.

In a way, you couldn't blame them. They tended to come more from rural areas and maybe had more of an adjustment to make to living in London – if someone from your village goes and lives halfway across the world and they're your mate, then if you do the same thing, it's inevitable you're going to want to join them. And under the pressure of trying to establish yourself in a new environment – especially when what makes you different is visible to all – it's only natural to close ranks. Looking back now, I can understand the fears they must have had, but there were fears on both sides – fear of losing jobs to people who would work longer hours for less money, fear of the manor you'd lived in all your life being taken away.

Going back to East and West Ham now, they're not just 'cosmopolitan', they're probably more Bangladeshi and Indian and Pakistani than they are anything else. The positive thing I can see happening in the playground of my old school is that maybe the younger generation are kind of educating us. Whether one side is becoming more Anglicised or the other is becoming less so – or most likely a bit of both – what they've got to do is learn to meet in the middle.

Whatever happens, it's probably not going to be anything that hasn't happened along the banks of the River Thames plenty of times before. The other side of all those dockyard traditions that have always given the inner London section of the East End its exotic edge is that it's also always been the place that immigrants have come to first, whether that's meant the Huguenots or the Chinese or the Jews or the Hindus or the Muslims or the Poles or the Romanians. The docks might be gone now, but the tide still goes in and out.

CHAPTER 5

THE NEW
LANSDOWNE CLUB

The years just before and after our move away from Plaistow are marked out in my mind by three huge moments in football history. In May of 1964, West Ham won the FA Cup for the first time ever. Dad, Mum, Laura and I walked down the bottom of Caistor Park Road (in those days you could still get straight out onto Plaistow Road) for the parade.

They couldn't even afford a double-decker. West Ham's idea of an 'open-topped bus' in those days was sitting on the roof of a coach, but that didn't stop us having a great time. We blew all our bubbles and had a little party afterwards. You don't get many days like that (at least, West Ham fans don't) so it's best to make the most of them when they do come around.

A year later, the good times miraculously continued as West Ham won the UEFA Cup Winners' Cup at Wembley. My dad had been thinking of getting us tickets for that one, but sadly decided not to take me with him in the end because he thought I was a bit young to be in such a big crowd (he probably had a point, as almost a hundred thousand turned up to see us beat Munich 1860 2–0). We were only the second English team to win that competition. I can't remember who the first mob were.

Luckily, by the time the World Cup came round a year later, my dad had decided that at nine I was now old enough for Wembley. So he called in some favours from people he knew in the fruit and veg trade and we ended up getting tickets to every game England played. Full match reports are coming later in this chapter for anyone who doesn't know how the tournament ended. But before that, there's another landmark to be negotiated – nothing to rival Bobby Moore bringing the World Cup home in terms of historic significance, but an event which probably defined the course of the rest of my life.

If the Winstones had just stayed in Plaistow, that probably would've been it for me for the duration. But in the year between those two Wembley finals our family had made a move which brought us much closer to the twin towers, but took us what felt like a long way from the place I'd always thought of as home (and probably continue to think of that way, despite all physical evidence to the contrary). It's not like my dad sat us down and told us we were moving to Australia – it was only Enfield, or to be more precise 336 Church Street, on the Winchmore Hill side of the A10 – but it might as well have been the furthest shores of the Antipodes as far as I was concerned.

North London is a foreign country, they do things differently there. I couldn't really even book Enfield as being in London, any-way (it is now, but then it felt more like Middlesex). From being a kid with a very clear idea of who I was and where I belonged, I sud-denly found myself moving to another place where the only things anyone at my new school knew about me were that my accent was different, I didn't really have any friends, and I seemed to be a couple of years behind where I should've been with my education.

I don't think I was fully dyslexic, but when I wrote something my eyes tended to move around the page, and I'd have to check over what I'd done at the end to make sure that the thought which had left my mind had actually reached the paper. It's the same with emails even now – I have to go through them at the end to make sure I haven't got distracted and left something out. I wasn't a great one for reading at school, either, and it's probably only having to learn scripts that has brought my spelling up to a level where I can just about get by.

As a defence mechanism to protect me from the things about my new life that I was finding difficult, I became a bit of an inverted snob. In my eight-year-old mind, I was a proper Plaistow geezer and all this country-bumpkin business wasn't for me, but that probably made life more difficult rather than easier. It's hard for any kid to move away from their mates and everything they know and love, and when you go into school for the first few times, you just feel like an alien. I'm not saying I know what someone who comes here from Poland or Pakistan goes through, because obviously the language is more of a factor there (although they do talk funny in Enfield), but if there'd been a ready-made community of East End kids for me to join up with at my new school, I'd have been in there in the blink of an eye.

I know what you're thinking: 'Enough of this bollocks about you being a sensitive cockney flower that should never have been transplanted up the A10, Ray, just tell us about the football.' The great thing about going to the 1966 World Cup was that even though my dad managed to get two tickets for every game, he made it a surprise every time. It was really good of him to take me because deep down he wasn't even that much of a football fan – he'd supported Arsenal when he was younger, so he can't have been.

A lot of people of my age or older will tell you that their memories of these matches are in black and white, because that's how they saw the games on TV at the time. My recollections are a strange mixture of Technicolor from actually being there – the light blue of Uruguay's kit, or the green of Mexico's – overlaid with the monochrome of endless subsequent viewings. The commentaries have seeped in too at some key moments, even though I only heard them afterwards.

The first game was Uruguay at Wembley. Geoff Hurst didn't play, but I've got a feeling Greavesie did. He was a fantastic player, and we had Terry Payne from Southampton on the wing, but that didn't stop it being a boring 0–0. England weren't expected to do too much in the World Cup and Uruguay were a tough nut to crack.

The one thing I'll never forget about that day is, you know how at the beginning of the game they'll have all the teams coming out represented by schoolchildren as mascots? With the World Cup now it'll be all fireworks going off and balloons going up, someone sings a song and it's a big show. But then it was just a few kids coming out with sticks – like people would use to make a banner for protesting outside an embassy – with the name of the team written at right angles on a piece of wood.

My dad bought me a 'World Cup Willie' pennant and also a West Ham one which I've still got to this day. With those lucky charms in place, the following two games went much better. Bobby Charlton scored a screamer against Mexico, and Roger Hunt got one too, then Hunt scored both our goals against France.

Next up were Argentina. Geoff Hurst played in that one and Antonio Rattín got sent off. We did well to hold our tempers as Argentina were scrapping like animals, but then Bobby Moore put the ball down quickly and flicked it up for Geoff Hurst to nut it in, and Argentina were history. It was almost like a dress rehearsal for our first goal in the final. By then a measure of optimism had really started to take hold, but Eusébio's Portugal were still favourites to knock us out in the semis. They were blitzing everyone, but Geoff Hurst and Bobby Charlton both scored and now England were in the final.

When that great day came I had more than a vague idea of what being 1–0 down to the German machine meant, because I could still feel the clip round the earhole I'd got off the copper for playing in one of the bombsites they'd left. There was a lot of historical friction and a real sense of them being the old enemy, so going 2–1 up just set you up for the emotional sucker punch of them equalising. I remember almost crying when they pulled that goal back – which wouldn't have been the done thing then, although you see dads do-ing it as well as kids on *Match of the Day* all the time now.

The sense of pride when we finally did them at the end of extra time was amazing (that's where the voice of Kenneth Wolstenholme butts in, even though I wasn't listening to him at the time), especially as three of the most important members of the team – the cap-tain Bobby Moore, Geoff Hurst who scored a hat-trick and Martin Peters who scored the other goal – were West Ham heroes. To see Bobby Moore holding up the trophy with his chest puffed out at the end of that gruelling game was an experience I'll never forget.

The funny thing is that when you're nine years old, the euphoria of actually being World Champions seems perfectly natural. We're British and we won the war, so it's sort of expected that we should win the World Cup as well. Forty-eight years later, I can look back on that feeling from a more worldly-wise perspective. I suppose the era I was brought up in was basically the end of the British Empire, but we still felt like a force in the world. We had The Beatles, we had the World Cup. We were kind of alright.

Times were still hard for a lot of people, but the economy was doing pretty well. Our family's improving situation was probably a good example of the way people from working-class backgrounds could get on in the mid-sixties. Although I was pissed off to have had to leave Plaistow, I had a lot to be thankful for.

We'd moved into a really nice four-bedroom George Reid house. My parents had paid four and a half grand for it, which was a lot of money at a time when the average weekly wage wasn't much more than £16. It was the equivalent of buying a house for £750,000 today, which was obviously a bit of a stretch, but my mum and dad were, for the moment at least, on a much sounder financial footing than they had been. On top of that, they'd gone thoroughly legit.

Ever since the nasty incident in Walthamstow with the Kray brothers, my dad had backed away from the ducking-and-diving side of things. That can't have been easy, because there was quite a romantic image to it in those days, but I think there comes a time when you've got a family that you don't want to be shitting yourself every time there's a knock on the door. He stepped back from all the other bollocks and concentrated on going to work, to the point where he'd been able to step up to running his own grocer's.

His first shop was in Bush Hill Parade, just outside Enfield, which was why we ended up moving there. The impetus for the move came from Mum. She'd got Nanny Rich's genes after all. Whereas my dad – no disrespect to him – was quite set in his ways, and if left to his own devices might have been happy staying in a council flat in Hackney all his life. Although I didn't know this at the time, my sister told me recently that my mum just sold our home in Plaistow without asking him. Some blokes came around making offers on a lot of people's houses for buy-to-let and she just turned it over to them and went off and picked out the house in Enfield without saying a word to Dad. Then again, if she had asked him, he probably would've said no.

Either way, Mum was the motivator, and even though I wasn't too happy about the move at the time, there was no denying we'd gone up in the world. We had a nice bit of garden now, and after we'd been in Enfield for a few years we got a bar installed in the front room – the forerunner of Raymondo's, whose doors are still always open in my house to this day – with one of those Bobby Moore World Cup ice buckets. Everyone had one of those, or at least every West Ham fan did. Bobby was standing on the brown-coloured ball holding the World Cup, then you'd lift him up and all your ice would be in there.

We got a dog as well. He was a Boxer (I suppose that ran in the family) called Brandy. He was soppy as a bag of bollocks with us – you could do what you liked with him – but if anyone else came within range, he'd mullah 'em, even when he got so old he only had one tooth left.

They say your porn name is your first pet and the first street you can remember, which makes mine 'Brandy Caistor'. I reckon I'd do alright with that, then if I wanted to redefine myself as an actress and go a bit respectable later on in my career, I could always change it to 'Brandy Caistor-Park', which sounds much more distinguished. Brandy was a clever old bastard as well. The dustmen used to tease him in the alley where the bins were, so he worked out how to back up and make it look like his lead was tighter than it was, then when the dustman came to torment him, Brandy had him on the penny and gave him a right good biting.

When we'd lived in Plaistow, one of the things I'd liked do-ing best was driving over to Hackney to see Maud and Toffy on a Sunday. There were all sorts of different cars we'd go in – they weren't necessarily ours. In those days if you wanted a car, you just had one. You could do that then – thank God you can't any more, because I don't want anyone just taking mine. One of my dad's cars (well, I say it was his . . . we certainly used it a lot) – a black Ford Zephyr – ended up in a pond at Victoria Park once after someone had nicked it and used it on a blag.

We'd jump in the car (whichever one it was) all suited up and looking nice to go off and meet the cousins while Mum would stay at home and cook the dinner. Even the mums who wore the trousers had to miss out on a lot of fun in those days, on account of their place still being in the home. My aunties Irene, Barbara (Charlie's wife) and Joycie (Kenny's wife) would all be back in their kitchens cooking up a storm, while their kids Scott, Spencer and Becky, Charlie and Maureen, and Tracey and Melanie came down to Hackney to meet us.

We'd go up to the flats first to see Granddad and Nanny. Obviously she'd have to stay at home to cook the dinner as well, so it would just be Toffy who came down to the New Lansdowne Club with us. It was a proper old East End gaff – a working men's club with a snooker table and a boxing gym. My granddad had been on the committee so he had a lot of mates there, like Archie who could hit you with either hand. A few of them and maybe some of Charlie's pals would come and join us until there was quite a gathering.

All the fellas would have a drink and a chat and the kids'd be fucking about and getting up to mischief, messing around on the drumkit. Someone might even get up and sing a song – me and my sister would do 'Cinderella Rockefella' or Sonny and Cher's 'I Got You, Babe', and one of the uncles might give us a bit of Sinatra. Then we'd all head home in time for our separate Sunday dinners at three or four in the afternoon – there was never too much traffic on the roads on a Sunday.

I had a few tussles at the Lansdowne with my cousin Charlie's sister Maureen, who was a couple of years older than us and even trappier than I was. She's my cousin and I love her to death, but we did used to bicker a lot. That said, I remember one time when we were visiting her mum and dad in the Barbican, and me and Charlie were getting bullied by a gang of older kids, Maureen went and sorted them all out – shut them right up with a couple of swift right-handers. It's a good job she wasn't born a geezer because then she'd have been even more dangerous.

After we'd moved, being in Enfield exile made those weekly trips to the Lansdowne something to look forward to even more. It wasn't actually much further to bomb down the A10 than it had been to drive over from Plaistow, anyway, and going there to see all the family felt like going home. When I went back to have a look at the old place again recently the building was still there – walk south down Mare Street past the Hackney Empire and the town hall and it's on your right – but there were boards up all around it.

I'm hoping someone's got some Lottery funds to restore it, because I know it had fallen into serious disrepair. There were a load of depressing photos online showing how it had been squatted by some junkies who'd made a horrible mess of the place, but you could still see the beautiful interior underneath. If I had the money, I'd do it up myself.

CHAPTER 6

THE CAGE,
SPITALFIELDS MARKET

My new primary school in Enfield was called Raglan, and as I may already have mentioned – probably three or four times – I didn't like it much there at first. Things only began to look up once I got into the school football team. We were a pretty good little side and managed to get to a regional cup semi-final. We lost 2–1 in that but my mate Colin Bailey scored.

Even as young as nine or ten, I was already looking for any excuse to get back to East London. So when my dad asked me if I fancied getting up early and going down to Spitalfields Market with him before school, I jumped at the chance. It wasn't really to work at that age, it was more just to meet his mates – they'd all bring their boys down to see how life was and show them there's a great big world out there. This was at the time when he had the shop in Bush Hill Parade, so we'd be back for Dad to open it and for me to get to school. The other kids would be at home having their Ready Brek and I'd be down the market, drinking in the local colour – a commodity of which there was not a shortage, in fact 'colourful' is the politest word you'd use.

Spitalfields Market was as formative an educational experience as any boy could hope for. I used to shadow-box down there with a real gentleman called Sammy McCarthy, who had boxed as a pro and will turn up in the story again later on in somewhat less happy circumstances. There were a lot of old fighters around who my dad had known as kids, and I'd have a spar with them all. My dad's pal Archie Joyce's older brother Teddy would throw a few imaginary right hands for me to fend off, and that's when the 'Little Sugar' nickname really started to stick.

Another thing I loved down there was the special market coinage which you could only spend in A. Mays, the big shop on the corner. It came in triangles and 50p shapes, but before the 50p had even come out – I suppose they were tokens more than anything – and I saved loads of them when I was little. Until recently I still had thousands of them in boxes and tins in the garage that I was going to polish up and get framed, but then when I was having some work done at home the fucking geezer threw them on the fire and they all melted. I could've killed him.

The breakfast you'd have on that market early in the morning would taste better than you could get anywhere else on earth. To this day I still love a bacon roll – a good crusty white one with brown sauce in it – and the place we'd get them was the Blue Café. It's not there any more, but it was just up from Gun Street, along the south side of the market, and it was owned by Vic Andretti's dad Victor – we called him Uncle Victor. His son, who was a mate of my dad's, won a European boxing title, and gave me the gloves he wore, which still had the claret on 'em.

By coincidence it was outside Uncle Victor's café that I saw the longest street-fight I've ever seen in my life. Two fellas had what we used to call a 'straightener', which is like a formal stand-up bare-knuckle fight where someone's got a grievance and everyone backs off to let them sort it out. I know it sounds like I'm exaggerating – and I probably am a bit, because I was only a kid – but I swear this fight went on for twenty minutes. Now, that might not seem like a long time to you if you don't know anything about boxing, but if you think that even a fit professional fighter will be blowing after a three-minute round, then you can imagine that twenty minutes without a break feels like a lifetime.

Not that they didn't have the odd pause for breath, because when one of them knocked the other down, he'd stand and wait for his adversary to get back up. Every time someone got knocked over it was almost like the end of the round. There was no kicking anyone in the head or anything like that – it was all very courteous and old-fashioned. All the guys were standing round watching, and I was there with them, a small boy with a bacon roll.

By the time those two were done it didn't even seem to matter who won any more. At the end they both shook hands and went in the café to have a nice cup of tea, and everyone was clapping them and saying, 'Blinding fight.' Obviously this is a very romantic notion of what violence should be like, but that only made it more impressive to see it actually happen. In a strange way it was a beautiful thing to watch – two men just being men – but it was also pretty scary. I wasn't much more than ten years old at the time, and they were really going at it: I mean, this was a severe tear-up, but it was still some way short of being the most unnerving thing I saw happen in that market.

Across the way from the Blue Café was a place called 'the Cage', which was where all the big lorries pulled up to load in and load out. That was also where the methers – the tramps – used to burn the bushel boxes to keep warm. They'd all be sleeping around the fire in the winter with big old coats on. You don't see meths drinkers so much now – it's like it's gone out of fashion. I suppose they'd be crystal methers now. Maybe the news has finally broken that drinking methylated spirits is bad for you – I think the clue was in the way they coloured it blue and purple.

The meths drinkers used to have their own hierarchy, with different pitches and guv'nors who sometimes used to fall out among themselves and have a ruck. I don't know if it's still like that among the homeless today, but you're going to get that kind of thing going on wherever people are under pressure, and I don't suppose changing the intoxicant of choice will have ushered in a new era of peace and harmony.

My dad used to bring them in old coats and shoes sometimes, but you could guarantee that the next week they wouldn't have them any more, because they'd have sold them to buy meths. He wasn't the only one on the market who used to do this, either. Other people would bring them out a bacon sandwich or an egg roll. The methers did get looked after, they just didn't look after themselves.

I remember standing by the Cage once with my dad and Billy and Johnny Cambridge. They were two of his mates from over the water – not the Irish Sea, the Thames – and they used to have a painted cab with horseshoes on it. Quite a few of the South London greengrocers were a bit gypsy-ish, and the Cambridges were wealthy fellas and grafters with it. I remember Billy having a row with a one-armed mether once – the geezer pointed to the stump where his arm used to be and said, 'If I still had that, boy, I'd put it on ya!'

Anyway, Billy and Johnny were nice guys, from a really good family. And we were just standing there having a fag (well, the men were – I'm not sure I'd've been allowed one at that age) when an articulated lorry drove into the Cage without looking carefully enough and ran straight over one of the tramp's legs in his sleeping bag. The worst part of it was, this old boy was so cold and rotten with meths that he never even woke up. Hopefully that meant he didn't feel the impact, but it was a horrible thing to see – never mind hear. He was still alive when they took him away in the ambulance, but he was in for a nasty surprise when he eventually woke up. I've had some pretty serious hangovers in my time, but nothing on quite that level.

Spitalfields in the late sixties and early seventies was a rough, noisy old place, but it was definitely alive. When I first started going there I was only a kid, so I wasn't really old enough to understand the politics of it all. Everyone would make a fuss of you, but sometimes you'd get a sense that there was a bit of an edge to it when someone from a different firm came over.

I was walking down the market with my dad one day when a fella went to doff his cap to us. Bosh! My dad knocked him out. My jaw was on the floor – just like the other geezer's was, but for different reasons. I was thinking, 'What's he done that for?' But it turned out a lot of the lorry drivers from up North used to carry a razor blade in their cap, and if you crossed 'em they'd whip it out and cut you with it. Obviously something had gone on between them before and my dad needed to get his retaliation in first.

Apparently they used to hide razors in their lapels as well, so if you grabbed their jacket and went to nut them, the blade would cut your hands to pieces. I think it's an old Teddy Boy thing, but the lorry drivers used to do it too. All sorts of nasty things could happen if you got on the wrong side of the wrong people in that market. I never saw this done myself but I heard about people getting their legs held down across the kerb and broken the wrong way, or someone getting a pencil through their eardrum. It wasn't like there was any reason for that to be happening to me, but the fact that some real tough guys worked on that market was definitely a big part of the character of the place.

If you go to Spitalfields now, the atmosphere could hardly be more different. There are new shops, which certainly don't take triangular tokens, where A. Mays and the Cage used to be, and while there's still a market, it now sells clothes to tourists on one day and antiques or artworks on another. The basic layout of the whole covered section is pretty much unchanged, but it's all been tidied up so much that it's hard to believe it's the same place. It's kind of recognisable and unrecognisable at the same time – like a big crab shell that a smaller sea creature has moved into after the former resident has departed.

The same thing's happened at Covent Garden, the old fish market at Billingsgate was moved out to the Isle of Dogs years ago, and it won't be long till the meat market at Smithfield follows. Sometimes it's a shame things have to change. Many of those men I met at Spitalfields as a kid were members of families who'd passed stalls down from father to son since the time of Henry Mayhew's costermongers and before, and yet now all those traditions which have come down across the generations have disappeared.

I'm not one of those people who believe nothing new should ever be allowed to happen, though. And some of what went on in that place we're probably better off without. I never actually saw my dad come off worse in any of the tussles he had, but everyone does some time, and it's much better to be coming home from work without lumps and bumps all over you. I wouldn't want to paint a picture of him as someone who was constantly having rows, but those are the stories you tend to remember.

When my mind turns to happier times, there's a holiday in Bournemouth that always comes back to me, for some reason. One day – I think it was a bank holiday Monday – we got the boat across to the Isle of Wight. Dad was never great on boat trips and when we got to the other side where there was a coach waiting to take everyone round the island, he said, 'We're not getting on a coach, let's walk round the island.' He had no comprehension of how big it was – I think he thought it was like the Isle of Dogs – 'Of course we can walk round the Isle of Wight. It's a dot on the map to us. You get on your coach and we'll have a little bit of proper . . .'

We were only kids at the time, and the minute the coach drove off, the realisation hit us that this place was not only huge, it was also pretty desolate. What's more, nothing was open 'cos it was a bank holiday, so we were basically going to be stuck there for the next seven hours. As it turned out, we ended up having a blinding day. We found this little hotel which was willing to take us in and give us a bit of dinner. We played football and flew a kite. I think it was that make-the-best-of-it attitude that the English have when we're not moaning about everything which saw us through.

All nearly didn't end so well, though. We had the dog with us, and at one point we were walking along the top of some cliffs when Brandy came to a hole in the sea wall and jumped right through it. I looked over the edge and I could see him disappearing like in a cartoon – sailing through the air to land on his chin with his legs splayed out all around him. I knew he was dead – there was no way he could've survived that fall. But just like that indestructible Labrador on the Southend road a few years earlier, he got up, shook himself and found a path to run all the way back to us. It was fucking unbelievable – who did he think he was, Superdog?

Some other holidays I look back upon really fondly were with my nan and granddad. I was probably nine or ten when they took us to the Ocean Hotel in Brighton, which was like Butlins' flagship hotel. There was a fancy dress competition and I went as a billboard – it was my first big advertising job – while Laura was the Queen of Hearts. We watched *She Wore a Yellow Ribbon* at the cinema club in the afternoon (I've always loved John Wayne and I still think he's a very under-rated actor). And I remember Maud and Toffy dancing together in the evening – my granddad was a terrific dancer and loved spinning Nanny Maud round the floor.

A couple of years later – it must have been right at the end of the sixties – they took us on our first foreign holiday. We went to Arenal in Majorca, and I loved the freedom of being abroad right from the off. You can get the paella, but if you don't fancy it, they still eat egg and chips just like us. Granddad would still always have a tie on when he was on the beach – they would, the old guys, they always looked immaculate – and he couldn't pass a woman without lifting his hat, even if she was only wearing a bikini.

CHAPTER 7

RONAN POINT

Early on the morning of 16 May 1968, an old lady who'd recently moved into a newly built East London block of flats lit a match to get the stove going for her morning cup of tea. The gas explosion that followed sent her flying across the kitchen and left her shaken but miraculously unharmed. That should've been the end of it, but weaknesses in the just-completed building caused the whole south-east side of the block to collapse with a human toll – four dead and seventeen injured – that would have been much higher if most of the flats hadn't still been unoccupied.

This disaster made a huge impression on me at the age of eleven because it happened on our old patch – just down the road from Plaistow, on the way to Custom House. Looking back, I can see it also had a wider significance. It was certainly poetic justice that the block concerned had been named after a former chairman of Newham council's housing committee (I didn't know that at the time, I just Googled it), because the now infamous Ronan Point became a symbol of the huge mistakes that were made back then in building the new accommodation that East London, and Britain as a whole, so desperately needed.

We wanted homes building – and quickly – but instead of houses, they gave us prisons in the sky. I realise that some of the architects and town planners responsible were probably quite idealistic people, but it was easy for them to be idealistic when they didn't actually have to live in these places. Those gaps where the bombsites were should have been filled with the kind of properties that would have enhanced the communities that already existed. Instead, whole streets of perfectly good houses were demolished and everyone was shipped off into these fucking great big concrete tower blocks.

Not only did these new high-rise buildings split up communities and separate people from the neighbours they'd lived with all their lives, they also – as the Ronan Point disaster demonstrated – weren't very well built. However idealistic some of the original plans might have been, a lot of the good intentions got lost in the transition from two-dimensional drawings to three-dimensional reality. It wasn't just government cost-cutting that did the damage, there was a lot of skulduggery going on as well, with a lot of the money going into the wrong people's pockets via the old secret handshake.

Obviously this wasn't bothering the Winstone family too much in our nice new house in Enfield, but when I'd go back to Plaistow to visit my old mates, I could feel the landscape changing. My memories of growing up there were very much low-rise – you could see the sky, it wasn't all huge blocks looming up over you, and there was much more of a village mentality. But once they started turfing people out of their old terraced houses and moving them into these new flats, no one knew who lived next door to them any more. Sometimes it almost felt like a divide-and-conquer thing.

Going back there started to get depressing as more and more people moved on. The last time I went back there on a Red Bus Rover I was probably thirteen. By that time I only had one mate left living on Caistor Park Road. His name – and I'm not making this up – was Micky Ghostfield. A field of ghosts was what that place was starting to feel like to me, and when I went back to knock for him, the fucker lived up to his name by blanking me. He might as well have answered the door with a white sheet over his head. I guess he hadn't seen me for a while and didn't want to know. I suppose I can understand it in a way, but then again, if you're reading this, Micky, fuck you.

One place out East I never got tired of going was Shoeburyness. In the summer holidays we would basically be shipped off there for six weeks. My mum would come with us and then my dad would drive down for the odd weekend because he'd be working. I remember going up the OAPs' club with my nan quite a lot. Sometimes me and my sister would get up and do a song to entertain the troops. You've got to have your party piece, and we had some great parties at home and at our aunties' and uncles' houses at that time, when everyone would get up and sing.

After a few years in Bush Hill Parade, my Old Man progressed to a bigger shop up in Watford. My dad was always known for having a great flash. I'm not being personal, that's what they called the display of produce you'd use to entice the punters into your shop. The apples would all be beautifully polished, and he found a way of putting mirrors in at the back of the shelves to make the fruit look massive, so people would come in just to look at it. It was like fruit and veg CGI.

As his operation got bigger his overheads would've gone up too, but as kids we never felt we were going without anything. He must've felt pressure to pay the bills and put food on the table, and we could tell by the way he walked up the front path if he'd had a bad day. He didn't get the hump with us as much as with himself, but I remember one night when he came home and we'd already got the message that he was in a bad mood. Then Mum put his dinner on the table and he just threw it straight out the window.

There is an anger in our family, which for my part I like to think I've learnt to control much better these days, but it's taken me a long time. We're argumentative and stubborn and tend to have short fuses. My mum was the exception to that – she was very good at letting Dad have his tantrum while never letting there be too much doubt about who the real boss was. They did have rows, but it never got physical or violent.

Well, I suppose it depends on how you define violence. Some people think shouting and screaming or throwing things is violent, but I don't. It's what you're used to, isn't it? If you live in a quiet house, then someone raising their voice can be more shocking than a full-scale barney would be somewhere else. I think our way of doing things was quite healthy, really, because nothing got bottled up. There'd be a huge slanging match and next thing you knew we'd all be on the sofa, hugging each other and crying at the Sunday afternoon film.

My dad only properly hit me once in my life, when I was caught cheating in a school exam. I had done it, so they'd got me bang to rights. I came home from school to see the letter on the mantelpiece, so I had it on my toes rather than face the music. Obviously that only made the situation worse. By the time I finally got up the courage to go back home it was about ten o'clock at night. My dad opened the front door, and before he'd even finished asking me where the fuck I'd been, he'd gone bosh, and chinned me. I probably deserved it, and the message his punch delivered has certainly stuck with me: 'If you're not good at it, don't fucking do it.' That's a very pragmatic moral code: not 'don't do it because it's wrong', rather 'don't do it because you're not good enough at it not to get caught'.

Now that I think about it, this was probably a bit later on, maybe more into my mid-teens, but I might as well do the other big family row while I'm at it. There was another incident when my mum and dad were having a barney and I thought I was becoming a man so I should probably intervene. I stepped in and said, 'Why don't you leave her alone?' But it wasn't my dad who reacted – he just looked at me as if to say, 'You really don't know what you've done here' – it was my mum. She didn't just tell me to mind my own business, she threw the gin and tonic she had in her hand at me to underline the point.

I think she'd have hit me with it if she'd wanted to, but the glass smashed against the door close enough to my head to send me ske-daddling out the door. I'm getting quite into these stories now, but maybe I should save the one where my sister stabbed me with a fork for a bit later on.

The fact that I've gone on so far ahead of myself in time probably gives you a fair idea of how interested I was in my secondary school. Because I was still quite different to a lot of the other kids there, in terms of how I talked and how I carried myself, I did get picked on a little bit. At that point, if you're not going to be someone who gets bullied throughout your time at the school, you have to kind of design a way to survive. Whether that means having a fight and taking a belting, or just trying to stay out of certain bigger kids' way is up to you.

When I first went to Edmonton County, a big change in the British education system had just shifted it from a grammar school to a comprehensive. On a practical level, this meant kids who wanted to learn were suddenly finding themselves in classes with kids who didn't. No prizes for guessing which side of this line I was usually on. On the downside, this meant I could now experience the dubious pleasure of holding my brighter classmates back. On the upside, contact with kids who saw things a different way to how I did would actually have a beneficial impact on me.

There was one boy called Stewart West, who was a big dumpy kid and a bit of a schoolboy philosopher. He said something once which really stuck with me, about life and death being like a cassette tape: once you get to the end it rewinds and plays again. I haven't explained it as well as he did, and at the time I had absolutely no idea what he was talking about, but it certainly left an impression.

Now I think about it, maybe someone had taught him the idea of reincarnation – perhaps his parents were Hare Krishnas. Either way, this was something that caught my interest, and it fed into the two subjects at school that I'd really started to get into, which were history and physics. I ended up getting more than ninety per cent in the end of year exams in those subjects because I liked them so much.

Obviously history and physics is quite an unusual combination, and my enthusiasm for them didn't stop me being shit at chemistry and geography. The reason I paid more attention in those classes was mainly because we had great teachers in them. Mr Povey, who was the physics teacher, was one of those mad professor types who capture your attention by being as nutty as a fruitcake. He threw a kid called Chamberlain out the first-floor window once, just to see what would happen.

I was not immune to the joy of doing things for that reason myself. The Enfield ABC, which was the cinema where I went to the Saturday morning pictures, used to get a load of young rockers in, sitting downstairs. Me and my mates would lurk up in the circle, pouring drinks down on them over the balcony and generally causing murders. They'd try and run up the stairs to get us but we'd have it on our toes before they could catch us.

The other big draw at the Saturday morning pictures was that every week would be your birthday. OK, maybe not quite every week, but they had this thing where if it was your birthday you would get called up onstage and be given candyfloss. I've always had a bit of a sweet tooth and I really liked candyfloss so I made sure I had as many different birthdays as possible under a variety of different names. I suppose I'd bought that East Ender's scamming culture with me to a certain extent – either that or I was already testing the boundaries of my dramatic range.

There was another cinema in Tottenham called the Florida which operated an unofficial open-door policy. Well, I say they operated it, really it was the creation of a new mate of mine called Alan Hewitt. This kid could climb anything – we used to call him Thomas O'Malley after the streetwise one in Disney's *The Aristocats*. We'd be about four- or five-handed, and Thomas would shin up a drainpipe round the back, in through a window and down to open the exit door and let us in. The Florida still got our pocket money in the end, we just got some sweets for it.

The cinema was still a big deal at that time, but TV was starting to make more of a fight of it. *Steptoe and Son* was quite popular in our house, and I remember pestering my mum and dad to be allowed to stay up to watch Roger Moore as Simon Templar in *The Saint*. I didn't even particularly like the programme, but I'd beg to watch it just so I could stay up a bit later on a Sunday night. Somehow the counter-argument, 'No, you've got school in the morning', never quite swung it for me.

The first colour TV in the family was my granddad's. He got it just in time for the 1970 Cup Final. Chelsea versus Leeds at Wembley was a bruising encounter (it finished 2–2, with Chelsea eventually winning the replay) and now we could see those bruises in all the colours of the rainbow. That was when football was football. Norman 'Bites yer legs' Hunter and Ron 'Chopper' Harris – they wouldn't have nicknames like that now. The sponsors of the Premier League would never allow it.

CHAPTER 8

RAYMOND'S TAILORS, LOWER CLAPTON

Every year in the run up to Christmas we'd go to my dad's tailor to get some clothes made. You had to have a special bit of clobber made for Christmas and Easter – it's something I still do today.

This geezer's shop was up beyond the north end of Mare Street, past the centre of Hackney that you have to drive round instead of through now, going towards Clapton Pond. I went back to have a look for the exact place recently but the shop was gone. I'm pretty sure the guy who owned it was called Raymond though, so when me and my dad came round we were three proper little Rays of sunshine.

One particular time we were in there – it was when I was getting my first pair of long trousers made (so I must've been in my very early teens, as we mostly used to be in shorts before then) – I remember my dad buying a very smart but conservative suit, the kind of thing Sean Connery used to wear as James Bond. My choice was a little more flamboyant. I had a pair of grey flannel trousers made for me, along with a blue mohair blazer that had my initials embroidered on the pocket. My middle name, which I never use, is Andrew, so the initials spelt out R.A.W, which looked pretty good, though I say it myself. If your name is Colin Roland Arthur Patterson, I would advise you to give this gimmick a wide berth.

My dad was always a snappy dresser, and I guess some of that rubbed off on me. When he was younger, he had a little bit of a quiff thing going on with his hair. He was never a Teddy Boy or anything, but that kind of Edwardian style sent its roots quite deep. That didn't mean there wasn't room for the odd moment of experimentation, though. I've got a great picture from the late fifties or early sixties somewhere (which sadly I've not been able to find to put in this book) of my dad and his mates all done up in these stripy jumpers with tapered trousers and pointy shoes.

They saw a fair bit of dirt in their working lives (especially the ones who worked on the fish market, who would definitely need to come home and have a scrub up at the end of the day, because the smell was terrible) but when they went out at night they were immaculate. You'd never know they'd even been to work, let alone lugged sides of beef or bags of potatoes or big vats of mackerel about since the early hours of the morning. I suppose that's half the point, really. You'll often find it's people who keep their hands clean all day who don't feel the need to worry too much about how they look in the evening.

It wasn't just my dad and his mates' fashion sense which harked back to Edwardian times. Their emotional lives had the same buttoned-up quality that their clothes did. To put it in a nutshell, they didn't let a lot go. This wasn't so much the case when I was little, when my dad was happy to be quite affectionate and even tender. But I remember a very clear cut-off point when I reached a certain age and the hugging stopped. I suppose you get to thirteen or fourteen and suddenly your balls drop and you become a man, and men don't cuddle each other (or at least they didn't in the early seventies). So one day your dad would get hold of you and give you a squeeze, and the next day he wouldn't.

This is an experience that a lot of men of my generation – or at least, a lot of the men I know – seem to remember. That's probably why now we're older we like to get hold of our mates and give them a cuddle, because we're trying to fill that gap. This doesn't always apply in other cultures, though. I say that because of an unfortunate incident with a younger American actor I was working with a few years back. I won't name him, because he's a big star and that would be a bit unfair, but it wasn't Leonardo DiCaprio. Oh alright, then, it was Matt Damon.

A lot of different people I'd worked with had told me about him, saying what a great kid he was, and he is a great kid – don't get me wrong – but I'd heard so many good things about Matt that when I met him, I felt like I knew him, so I gave him a big hug and said, 'Hello, kid, how are you doing?' and he went as stiff as a fucking board. I said, 'Oh, OK.' I guess I'd kind of got into his space – which is an unusual thing for an Englishman to do to an American, because they're notorious for doing it to us – but the poor fucker nearly had a heart attack. He probably thought I was trying to roger him.

There's a lot to be said for the modern way of doing things, where people are more open about their emotions, though. Especially when it comes to being a dad. Because sometimes as a kid you see things that trouble you, and if you can't talk about them, they play on your mind.

I'm not saying I'm bad luck to be around but, as I've mentioned before, I've seen a number of people killed or injured, especially in car accidents. It always seems to happen when I'm on the plot. There was one time when I was up in Southgate, helping my dad sell stuff out of a lorry. I must've been in my early teens, and I'm doing one side of the road for him, knocking on doors and saying, 'Hello, we've got this or that to sell', whatever it was. I've finished my section of the street, so I'm coming back down the road to find my dad, but I can't see him anywhere.

At this point I have a little sit-down on a low wall by a junction – one of those ones where it's almost like a roundabout but it ain't a roundabout – and I'm going into a bit of a daydream about what a nice area it is and what it would be like to live there. At this point a car comes down the road, but when it gets to the curved bit it never slows down. Well, it tries to at the last minute, but it's too late by then.

The car clips the kerb, and I know things are pretty serious be-cause everything goes into slow motion, like that time when Laura and I saw that woman's body slide out of the car when we were on our way to Southend. The car takes off – not high enough to be ac-tually flying, but certainly as high as in the film *Bullitt* – and as it goes flying through the air, the boot opens and the spare wheel falls out and starts bouncing down the road. Even as that's happening, the car smacks against a wall – there are bricks everywhere – and a woman's thrown out of the passenger side where the door's burst open. I can see her arm's bent round under her back at a bad angle, and even as I'm noticing that, what remains of the car comes flying back from where it's hit the wall and rolls over on top of her.

All this hasn't taken more than a couple of seconds. At this point, the guy who was driving, who seems to be OK, gets out and runs round to the other side of the car looking for the place where she's fallen. I'm trying to shout out, 'She's stuck underneath!' but I can't actually speak. I suppose I'm in shock – I was only a kid at the time.

I want to go and help but basically I'm still rooted to my spot on the wall thinking, 'Fuck me!'

Before I've even had the chance to get myself together the guy – all on his own, it was amazing the strength that came to him in a crisis, because he wasn't a big man – somehow lifts the car up and pulls her out from under it. By that time I've finally regained the power of movement, so I run up to him asking if they're alright. At this point, my Old Man turns up, sees what's happened, and instead of getting involved or seeing if there's anything we can do to help, he takes me straight up the road, puts me in our motor and we're gone.

It's what's called a 'stoppo' – where your first priority is to get the hell out of there. He said it was because he could see I was in shock, but I thought afterwards maybe we were selling something we shouldn't have been and he didn't want me to get in trouble as an accessory. Either way, the right moment never came up to ask my dad why he did what he did, even though I would've liked to know.

I was lucky that just at the point in my life where I maybe needed a bit of guidance – something to set me on the right road – boxing came along. Given that my dad and my granddad had both boxed before me, and my dad's mates had been calling me 'Little Sugar' and mock-sparring with me for pretty much as long as I could remember, it was inevitable that I was going to give it a go at some point. What I could never have predicted was how much I would take from it into the rest of my life. I honestly think I learnt more that was useful to me from boxing than I did from over ten years in the British education system (though I'm not blaming my schools for that – it was my doing more than anyone else's).

Something happens to a boxer when they get in the ring that changes their whole lives. I think it's mostly that you're frightened, and in the process of having to overcome that fear you find a deeper humanity in yourself. Everyone is scared when they step through those ropes – I don't care who you are, even Muhammad Ali used to be – because you know you're going to get some pain, and if that doesn't frighten you, you're a psychopath. But what boxing gives you is an understanding of your own capacity for fear, and a structure within which to deal with it.

Beyond that, it's not just the discipline of boxing which stands you in good stead, it's the morality: the respect you have first for the people who are training you, who you really don't want to let down, and then for your opponents. I've transferred so much from that into acting, where you've got to have respect for whoever's playing opposite you, because you can only be at your best if you're bringing the best out of them too. When I've talked before about the parallels between boxing and acting, people have sometimes thought I'm seeing other actors as my competition, but they're not the opposition you've got to find a way to overcome (well, not usually – all that scene-stealing stuff doesn't happen nearly as often as you might think), your adversary is the script.

When I was growing up, I often heard it said that when you come from the East End you talk about boxing and birds, but when you come from North London you talk about football and birds. I don't know how true that is in general, but I took my first tentative steps in the fight game as an East Londoner in exile at the New Enterprise boxing club in Tottenham. It was a good club, despite its unfortunate location in the heartland of an inferior football team.

I went along with a couple of guys from my school, Charlie Woods and Jeff Coward. They were both better boxers than me. Not just technically, they were much fitter as well. I was a skinny little runt – a long way from the more expansive frontage I offer the world today – and the first time you walk into a gym as a raw kid of twelve years old and see a load of grown-up fighters training, there's something wrong with you if you don't feel at least slightly intimidated. I remember a big boxer at that gym at the time was a black kid called Battleman Austin. I know, it's a great name, isn't it? More like something out of a Marvel Comic than an actual person.

Luckily for me, Battleman was up in the heavier weights (he was more of an Austin Maxi than an Austin Allegro), so there was no danger of me having to fight him. And obviously they don't just put the gloves on you and throw you out there the moment you arrive. They have a look at you first to see how you shape up, and then you're in the ring, sparring. That's the moment when you find out the difference between messing about with your dad's mates down the market and doing it for real.

Jeff Coward, the first kid I ever properly sparred with, is one of the many people I met through boxing who I still see today (when he comes back from Cyprus, where he lives now). His granddad, who my granddad knew, was Charlie Coward, a very brave man who was famous for having smuggled prisoners out of Auschwitz in the war and was later played by Dirk Bogarde in the film *The Password is Courage*. Not living down to their surname seemed to be a family tradition, as Jeff was as game as a bagel too.

Charlie Woods was the first person I had to have an actual formal boxing match with. It was only an exhibition bout, which means there's no decision at the end. That was probably good news for me, as I don't think I did too well. Number one, Charlie was still probably a better fighter than me at that point. Number two, he was my mate and I felt a bit weird about giving him a clump. It's a strange thing about the friendliness of the boxing world, that all the real camaraderie you share – and it's more real than any I've come across in any other walk of life, with the possible exception of the armed forces – is based on having to hit people who haven't actually done you any wrong.

Charlie was a lovely bubbly kid, and I was really sad a few years later when I heard he'd committed suicide. Another tragic young life gone, just like that lovely babysitter Sylvie. His body was discovered in a shed, where he'd covered himself with hay because he didn't want to be found. It was heroin that did it, and this would be the first time – but sadly not the last – I'd see what the effects of hard drugs can be. We'd kind of lost touch with one another by this time because he was in the drugs world and I wasn't. Obviously, people have to choose their own route through life, but there are some roads you really don't want to go down.

After I'd been going to the New Enterprise for about a year, I switched to a club in Enfield because it was nearer home. There was another kid from my school who went there who turned out to be a terrific fighter. His name was Chris Hall and he ended up as an ABA champion before becoming a trainer, which I think he still does today.

If you'd met this kid, you'd never have thought he was a boxing champion in the making. Not only was he very tall and gangly, but he was also quite a loner and had a tendency to hoard things. I remember him opening my ears to all these different kinds of music, though. It was bands like Yes and Genesis and Jethro Tull that he was into, and I remember thinking, 'Fucking hell, what is all this hippie shit?'

We'd never have listened to that kind of thing at school. It would've been considered more as music for posh people: 'We don't touch that. It's not for us, it's for kids who are going to university.' The funny thing is, now it only seems to be people who've gone to college who tend to progress in the music business, but in those days that was more of a stigma to be overcome. Maybe Chris was ahead of his time in that regard, but he was a really game fighter either way. Bam! Bam! Bam! He'd just march forward, and he was very hard to stop.

CHAPTER 9

THE REPTON
BOXING CLUB

A couple of years of training and fighting at gyms in Tottenham and Enfield probably did help cure me of some of my inverted snobbery about North London, but it couldn't stop me yearning to be back in the East End. I was thinking of switching to West Ham boxing club for a while, as that had a good reputation and it was on my old plot, but it would've been a big journey to do to get over there three times a week.

It was probably my dad who said, 'If you're going to box, you might as well do it at the Repton', which was much closer and easier to get to. Going there was the best decision I've ever made. Not only did it give me the chance to mix with champions on a regular basis, it also gave me a base back in the area I still thought of as home.

No disrespect to Enfield, but I always felt like a fish out of water there. The Jesuits do say, 'Give me a boy until he is seven years old and I will give you the man', and I'd lived in Plaistow till I was a year older than that, so it was no wonder I thought of myself as an East Londoner through and through. Obviously I live in Essex these days, but there are probably more East Enders of my age in that county than there are left in London. Everyone I knew when I was young seems to have moved out, and maybe once you realise that, you start to see it ain't the places you love so much as the people.

Moving from one boxing club to another is not like a transfer in football – no actual money changes hands – but you do have to sign forms and all that kind of stuff. The Repton was (and still is) definitely somewhere near the top of the premiership in boxing terms, so places there were quite sought after. I think you have to go through a three-week trial period before you can join now, but in those days the fact that I'd won a few fights in Enfield by that time probably got me in.

The Repton moved premises not long after I stopped boxing. It's now in the Gary Barker gymnasium in the old bathhouse on Cheshire Street, just east of Brick Lane. Darren Barker was a world champion whose brother, also a great fighter, was sadly killed in a car crash, so they named the new gym after him. The old place I used to go to was in Pollards Row, in the basement under the Bethnal Green Working Men's club. It's just a few hundred yards away. Go up Vallance Road – past the new house built on top of where the Kray brothers used to live at number 178 – do a right, then a left and you're there. Someone told me there's a vandalised Banksy on the wall outside now.

The first time I went to the Repton, my dad drove me. But given that I was thirteen or fourteen by then, I was soon old enough to get the train down to Bethnal Green from Lower Edmonton on my own. I used to love that journey – it really felt like going back home, and sometimes I'd be counting the hours till the time came to go. Even though it was a bit of a walk down Bethnal Green Road to the gym, through what was a rougher area in the early seventies than it is now, I never felt nervous or ill at ease about it. I didn't feel like I was entering potentially hostile territory, I felt like I belonged there.

As a young kid, the thing about Bethnal Green was its synony-mousness – is there even such a word as 'synonymousness'? I'm writ-ing a book now, so I feel I've got to stretch myself – with the Kray twins. Detective Superintendent Leonard 'Nipper' Read had finally got Ron and Reg banged up for the murders of George Cornell and Jack 'The Hat' McVitie in 1969, so even though they weren't physically around any more, the place still kind of smelt of 'em.

Whether this was right or wrong – after all, a lot of people did get hurt – they still had that aura about them of being Robin Hood characters. Hard evidence of the Krays robbing the rich and giving to the poor might have been hard to come by, but the mythology of 'nothing bad ever happened when the twins were about' (except the stuff they did, obviously) was still very powerful.

Now I'm a bit older and wiser, the idea that nobody ever broke into anybody's house in Bethnal Green in the sixties because Reg and Ronnie would sort them out is not one I really buy into any longer. But when you're young it's easy to get caught up in the romance of that way of thinking, and as far as people in general were concerned, I suppose another side of it was that when there's a bit of a reign of terror going on, it's only human nature to try to put a positive spin on it. I bet there are parts of Belfast where they'll still tell you you could leave all your windows open when the IRA were running things, however ridiculous the evidence of innocent people kidnapped and murdered might make that suggestion look.

One of the mistakes people often make when they talk about 'glamorising violence' is to think that this glamour is something that's only projected from the outside. It's on the inside as well. Just as it'd be crazy to assume policemen never watched *The Bill* or

The Wire (which I was going to be in originally, but I couldn't face the idea of living in Baltimore for six months of the year), so it is easy to under-estimate how much gangsters think about their public image. The traffic between myth and reality is not one way – life copies films almost as much as films copy life. And being a success-ful gangster is just as much of a performance as making it big in films is.

When you think about the way their interests overlap, it's no wonder there's such a big crossover between showbiz stars and the criminal underworld. Both sides need to get the balance just right between everyone knowing who they are and no one getting up in their face too much. That's why those relationships which used to shock everybody, say Barbara Windsor and Ronnie Knight or Diana Dors with Alan Lake, always kind of made sense to me.

The big stars in the sixties would always be in the clubs in the West End, and a lot of those clubs were owned by the Krays and whoever else was about. The glamorous people got looked after – 'cos obviously it's good business for the management if they're in your gaff – and all of a sudden they're in this world of intrigue and it's very exciting. The gangsters have got some style and they know how to turn on the charm. Plus anyone else gives you a problem and they're out on their ear sharpish.

With David Bailey and Diana Dors doing the business for them, the Krays couldn't have had better PR if they'd employed a firm (rather than simply being The Firm). And all these stories you'd hear about George Raft coming over and being with the boys and them having major connections in the States only kept the pot boiling even more. Obviously the pot was well and truly off the stove by the time I got to the Repton, but the reality that the twins wouldn't ever be cooking with gas in E2 again took a long time to sink in.

Luckily, joining the Repton gave me access to a glittering array of more suitable role models. Going down the stairs to the gym I'd look at the pictures on the wall and think, 'Every one of these boxers is a champion.' Looking back now, the Repton roll-call was amazing: Maurice Hope – Olympic champion, going to be a world champion; Billy Taylor – what a fighter!; Graham Moughton, captain of the Olympic team; John H. Stracey, another world champion; Johnny Whitehorn; Dave Odwell, another Olympic team captain . . . It was quite daunting to walk into the Repton and see those pictures, especially at first, but once I found my feet I soon realised how lucky I was to be at such a special club, because if you're training alongside these guys, you can't help but learn.

You walk down those stairs for the first time and straight away the place smells of blood, sweat and tears. What I didn't understand at the time was that a lot of the really important things the Repton was going to teach me wouldn't be about how to handle myself in the ring, they'd be about ethics – having respect for myself and having respect for humanity. It was only years later that I began to look back and think, 'Fuck me, I learnt a lot more than boxing.'

The boxing had to come first, though, and I had some great teachers there. The head coach was a guy called Tony Burns. Burnsy was the Repton, and for me he epitomises what's good about boys' club boxing trainers the world over. He never once trained you as a boxer – although he was more than capable of doing that – his greatest gift was as a matchmaker. A lot of them will overmatch you to try to move you up the ranks too fast, but Burnsy would always do his best to make any imbalance in your favour. If he thought there was any chance of you getting hurt, he just wouldn't put you in there.

Another guy I owe a lot to was Billy Howick, who taught me ringcraft, which is basically how to unbalance your opponent while staying within the law, or at least within the law in the referee's eyes. Billy's big thing was that if you make your opponent miss you the whole fight but you hit him once, then you've won the fight (I suppose he was the Sam Allardyce of his day in that regard). This always seemed pretty logical to me. Also at the Repton I was able to watch a lot of boxers like Dave Odwell and Billy Taylor, who were tremendous counter-punchers, so I styled myself that way too.

Amateur fights last for three rounds of three minutes each, which might not sound like much, but believe me it's long enough when someone's trying to hit you in the face from start to finish. Nowadays they force you to wear head-protectors, but I never did and I still wouldn't want to if I was starting out now. I think they make boxing more dangerous, rather than less. Head-protectors are there predominantly to stop you getting cuts, but the cuts aren't really the problem in terms of the long-term damage people sustain from boxing. It's the shaking of the head and thence the brain which is the worst thing.

If you haven't got a head-guard on, you can see everything. The most fundamental technique in boxing as far as I'm concerned is the slip and miss, which is the way you pull your head inside or outside your opponent's punches. Once you've put your head-guard on, you may have covered your brow and your chin, but at the same time you're a bigger target, so even when you slip, you're still getting hit. What that does is shake your head, which is the one thing you really don't want to happen. I've thought this for a long time and a lot of people agree with me, but unfortunately not the ones who make the rules. If it was down to me, I wouldn't even use head-guards for sparring. I think they do more harm than good even then.

A lot of the boys who started at the Repton around the same time as me I still see to this day. Among my group were: Billy Jobling, a great fighter who came out of the Isle of Dogs; Glenn Murphy, who became an actor on *London's Burning*; my mate Tony Yeates, who came over to the Repton from the Fitzroy Lodge club, which is south of the river; and a guy called Tony Marchant, who ended up as a writer. We had some brilliant moments together, and you don't keep people as friends for forty-odd years unless you have a special bond with them. For me it's a kind of moral code that they all share – boxing taught them to be old-fashioned gentlemen.

When the club was originally founded, in 1884, it was more or less a missionary outpost for the Derbyshire public school it was named after. The idea was to come to the East End, which at that point was considered a dangerous slum, and impart Victorian discipline to the lawless inhabitants by teaching them the Marquess of Queensbury's rules. Obviously there's a paternalistic element to that, but paternalism is not necessarily a bad thing. Especially when it gives you tools you can use any way you want. It was no coincidence that so many of my mates from the Repton went on to succeed in other fields, because our time there gave us psychological resources we could fall back on for the rest of our lives.

In a way, the impact the Repton had on us was very similar to the one Anna Scher's children's theatre (which she started up the road in Islington in the late sixties) was having at around the same time on another bunch of unruly Londoners – Ray Burdis, Pauline Quirke, Phil Daniels, Perry Benson, Tony London, Kathy Burke – many of whom are still my mates to this day. Anna would take kids who were maybe lacking a direction in life and getting in a little bit of trouble and give them something creative to focus on. The only difference was that she was doing it from a left-wing political perspective, which wouldn't have got you very far in the fight game.

Obviously people tend to think of a boxing club as a violent place, and the Repton's Latin motto, 'Non Viscera, Non Gloria' ('No

Guts, No Glory'), would do nothing to change their mind. But the club crest doesn't have a dove of peace with an olive branch in its mouth by accident, because one of the main things going there taught me was how to mix with a group of people as a unit, even as a community. Those who try to put boxing down as more brutal and less evolved than other pastimes have a hard time explaining away the fact that it was probably the first sport where there was no colour bar.

That's not to say Jack Johnson aka 'the Galveston Giant' had an easy time of it after becoming the first African-American world heavyweight champion in 1908. Obviously his marrying a white woman went down like a sack of shit, but no one could take away from him the fact that he had been World Champion. And when I think back to being fourteen years old in London in the early seventies – how things had changed over the course of a decade or so from the first time I saw a black man in the street who wasn't Kenny Lynch, to maybe a bit of a feeling of 'them and us' developing – I know how much I've got to thank boxing for. Because once you're mixing with people on the same wavelength, what used to be 'them and us' suddenly just becomes 'us'.

Boxing certainly showed football the way in terms of being the first truly integrated sport. In fact I think it's only just about catching up now. To say West Ham crowds did not always extend the friendliest of welcomes to visiting black players in the seventies would be putting it mildly, but at least we were the first British team ever to field three black players at the same time, when Clyde Best, Clive Charles and Ade Coker all played against Spurs in 1972.

I was at Upton Park a few years later to see West Brom's more celebrated black trio – Brendon Batson, Laurie Cunningham and Cyrille Regis – who the Baggies' then manager Ron Atkinson famously, if perhaps unhelpfully, dubbed 'The Three Degrees'. That day I saw one of the best examples I've ever seen of someone defusing a situation, which is not a skill I've always – if ever – had. Brendon Batson was down in the corner at the South Bank end when someone chucked a load of bananas on the pitch. He simply picked one up, peeled it, and ate it, and the whole stand clapped him.

That sort of thing used to happen all over the country, but Chelsea was the worst place I ever went for it – I suppose they've always been a bit less cosmopolitan in West London. Their fans used to call it 0–0 if one of their black players scored, 'cos a black geezer shouldn't be playing for them. His own fans! I remember going there with a mate of mine once when they were playing Leicester and a whole stand stood up and Sieg-Heiled. There were grown men of fifty doing it who were old enough to have fought in the war. It was fucking disgraceful.

Boxing was the first sport that, I believe, dealt with the problem of racism without even consciously approaching it; it approached itself, in a way. No one ever said, 'There will be no discrimination in boxing', it just kind of happened. I suppose because people were constantly in a one-on-one situation, or just training together in the gym, they couldn't help finding out, 'Hey, you're just like me.' Maurice Hope was older than me, but he was someone I really looked up to, and boxing opened up all our minds by sending us out into the world with a common identity to take with us.

CHAPTER 10

CHRISP STREET MARKET, POPLAR

When my dad had his grocer's shops – first in Enfield, and then in Watford – my mum used to come in and work with him. I'm pretty sure she lost a couple of kids during that time – not because she was working so hard, it was just bad luck. There was definitely one morning when she had to be taken home from the shop in Bush Hill Park because she'd miscarried, and I had a sense of it happening another time as well, even though it was never talked about. Dwelling on such things was not encouraged in those days, and even though she must have felt sadness about this loss, she never shared it with us.

The Old Man had a good spell with the shops and we lived well for a few years, but the fruit game was changing, with the supermarkets squeezing out everyone else. I was still only a kid but I think what made his business start to go tits up at the shop in Watford was when they put a new one-way system in so no one could park nearby any more. My dad probably hung in there for a bit longer than he should've done, because that shop was his pride and joy and

84

Now and then – outside 82 Caistor Park Road in 2014
and as a bouncing baby 57 years before.

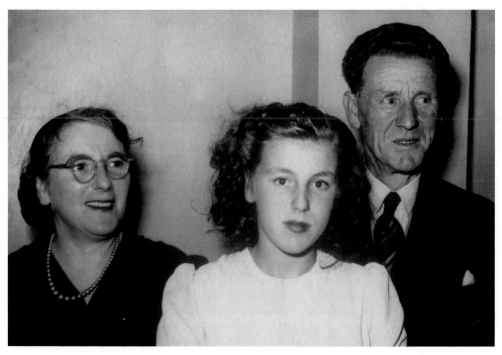

My mum with Nanny Rich and the first of her three husbands.

My mum and dad together before Laura and I came along.

Me posing on a blanket like a dog at Crufts.

At another wedding with my cousin Charlie-boy (I'm in the middle, he's on my right).
Not sure who the hatless kid was . . .

Cowboy-style this time in hat terms – with Laura in Nanny Rich's garden.

Early morning – the Cage with the sun rising in the east behind Christ Church, Spitalfields.

Old Spitalfields Market as it was – good luck finding a sack of King Edwards in there these days.

My dad looking suave on the market.

Spitalfields life before the clean-up, with The Cage, A. Mays and
Christ Church in the background.

West Ham bringing home the 1964 FA Cup on their luxury single-decker. All four of the Winstones are in that crowd somewhere.

Repton boys at the London Feds . . . (I'm the one bang in the middle).

With my dad after beating David Heyland (the tall one on the left) who was Essex champ. Although I won, I gave David the bigger trophy – winning was enough for me, and he was a nice kid.

Ready to rumble.

In *The Sweeney* in 1975, shortly before making my unauthorised escape.

Me in *Minder* – with George Cole on the right
and my fellow Corona old-boy Dennis Waterman between us.

he'd got a good living out of it. So in the end it totally ironed him out. He had no option but to go back out on the markets.

He had some mates who still had stalls so he started off working for them on various different markets – which wasn't something he'd had to do much before – until he got back on his feet. Me and Laura never went hungry, but there must've been a couple of years when the family was a bit financially challenged. My mum put a shift in too. She got a job collecting the money from fruit machines – not in a strong-arm kind of way, she was meant to be doing it – and inadvertently she taught me a useful scam.

On the old big machines, when you got a 'hold' you could fuse them out by pouring your Coca-Cola or lemonade over the buttons, and then they'd just carry on paying out until the machine was empty. This was something else I never looked upon as thieving. It's not as if the fruit-machine business is run on principles of good will to all men, anyway – it was just another kind of spillage. The money did come in handy, but you couldn't do it too often in the same pub, and sadly it doesn't work on the new machines . . . not that I've ever tried it, obviously.

The areas my mum was working in, mainly Hoxton and the bottom end of Islington, were quite rough at the time, so someone from the pub would usually escort her to the car. The sort of woman my mum was, if someone had come up to her and demanded the money, she wouldn't have been the one to risk her life by not giving them the bag. She'd probably have said, 'Here you go, son, take it', because money's not that important – at least, it's not when it's not yours. I guess there's always an element of danger any time you're collecting cash, but it's the cash that makes it dangerous, not the place you're picking it up. That said, in somewhere like Hoxton, life might actually be more dangerous for the person who's trying to nick it, because they don't know whose fucking place they're ripping off.

Returning to the markets was obviously a bit of a needs must for my dad. It wasn't a world he'd totally left behind, but he'd got pretty respectable with his shop in Watford and now he was having to go all over the place just to make a crust. Chrisp Street in Poplar is not necessarily somewhere you'd be setting up if you had any choice. But I was delighted, because I was old enough to go and help him now – on Saturdays, and maybe a day or two in the week sometimes as well – and as far as I was concerned, we were going home.

Obviously, you've got fewer overheads in that situation because you're just buying daily and selling what you can. Well, usually you're buying daily. If things are really tight, you might have to nick a bit of stock here and there to make up a deficit. I remember once we were a bit short of cash so we had to steal some tomatoes at Spitalfields Market. We had to have them away or we'd have had nothing to sell.

My dad kept the guy busy while I loaded the big old barrow with Canary tomatoes. Unfortunately I piled it too heavy at the back – I was only about fourteen at the time, and I suppose my eyes might've been bigger than my arm muscles. When the time came for me to have it on my toes, I came out of the market at top speed with the barrow behind me, hit the cobbled street, and the weight of it threw me what felt like twenty or thirty feet in the air. I seemed to be up there for ages – I was waving to the man in the moon – and by the time I finally landed in a heap with tomatoes splatting on the ground all around me I was lucky I hadn't burnt up on re-entry.

There would have been murders if we'd been caught, so we made as rapid an exit as possible, and I probably got a clip round the ear for my foolishness afterwards: 'If you're not any good at it, son, don't do it.' The way I was brought up was that if you owe someone some money and you're too skint to pay 'em back, you should usually front up and go and talk to them, but I suppose there were times when you have to find a way of earning the money to pay off the debt and you just have to do what you have to do. I remember us going to Covent Garden instead of Spitalfields to buy stock once or twice, which seemed perfectly natural at the time, but looking back it probably meant there were people on our usual plot we didn't want to run into.

These occasional incidents of ducking and diving probably gave me a head-start when the time came for me to play a gullible mechanic in *Minder* a few years later, but as a general rule my dad was no Arthur Daley. He was a grafter and he expected me to be the same, so when we arrived at Spitalfields at four in the morning there was a strict rule that we'd have to buy all our bits and get the lorry packed and tied up before we could stop for a nice cup of tea and a bacon roll.

Then we would head off to Chrisp Street or Roman Road or wherever we had a pitch and we'd have to pull the stall out and dress it. Cutting the cauliflowers was the worst job, especially in the winter. It used to get so cold that to this day I find I can't wear gloves in normal life, because if I put them on, my hands just start sweating.

Obviously, working on markets is no picnic. Sometimes you can stand around freezing your arse off all morning and come home with absolutely nothing. When I used to go to work with my dad, I knew that if we had a bad day I wouldn't get paid. Those were the rules of the job and I had no qualms about them. Well, I say that now – at the time I probably thought, 'Fuck it, I was going out tonight', but I knew that was the way things were done when you were part of a family business, and every now and then when you had a blinding day you would definitely get looked after.

The principle of 'fair's fair' also covered giving my mum house-keeping. 'Raymond, you've gotta do the right thing' were words drummed into me from an early age. Even if sometimes you borrowed it back by the end of the week, it was the gesture that counted – showing you knew you shouldn't take your food and lodging for granted, just because it was your parents who were giving it to you. My mum and dad shared that work ethic, and they've passed it on to me.

I remember falling back to sleep once after my dad had woken me up early to go to the market and getting a bucket of cold water thrown over me to make sure it didn't happen again. That gets you out of bed pretty sharpish, I can tell you, and it's another one of those childhood lessons that's stayed with me. I'm a stickler for time-keeping to this day. If I'm going anywhere I have to be punctual, if not early – it's almost an illness. And even if I've not gone to bed till four in the morning, I'll still be up with the sun. It's unheard-of for me to be asleep after nine in the morning.

Although as I said I was really pleased to be working at the market again, sometimes I used to moan about getting up early for work – especially if I'd got a bit of a hiding in the boxing ring the night before – but once we got there I loved getting to grips with the various personalities of the different markets we used to go to. Roman Road in Bow, for instance, was a funny old market, because it was only on Thursdays and Saturdays, not Fridays. It could be desolate there sometimes on a Thursday, especially because we were stuck at the Old Ford end, which is quieter than the Bethnal Green end.

We had a yard there just round the back of a little kids' clothes shop called 'Trendy', and there was a blinding old boy who used to work with us called Sammy Keyworth. I think he was Jewish and he'd make this kind of ehhh noise when he spoke, a bit like Blakey from *On the Buses*. One of my jobs at Roman Road was to take the orders to the other stalls. I'd have a big bag to carry with potatoes, carrots and cauliflowers on the bottom, softer fruit and veg higher up, and grapes on the top.

One time I'd taken them all up the road and delivered them when I saw from the look on my dad's face as I returned that I must've taken them to the wrong people. As I turned to walk away and give him a chance to cool down, a cauliflower hit me full bore on the back of the head. I was laid out sprawled across the middle of Roman Road – I know cauliflowers aren't normally thought of as weapons of mass destruction, but you know about it when one of those fuckers hits you on the canister. It was a bit harsh, but I never made the same mistake again, and I'll always have these two cauliflower ears to remember it by.

There was a nice girl who worked on one of the other stalls. Our eyes used to meet across the Roman on a regular basis, but I was a bit too shy to talk to her. Then I met her one night out and about somewhere and we had a lovely little evening together. It was weird though, because the next time I saw her on her stall we both went back to being exactly how we had been before. We liked each other too much to actually have a conversation.

Rathbone Market in Canning Town was a rough old place – not much chance of romance there, especially as our pitch was opposite the fish stall. Luckily we didn't hang around for too long, although I used to like the fact that we still knew a few people in that manor, because it was just down the road from Plaistow.

Chrisp Street in Poplar was a bit further from where we used to live, but that didn't stop it becoming my gateway to Upton Park. We used to work there quite regularly with Terry Brown, who was one of my granddad's tic-tac mates. All those families knew each other, and me and Terry's son Billy would take it in turns to go up to the Boleyn Ground for West Ham home games. I'll save that for the next chapter though, to give fans of lesser teams a chance to prepare themselves for the thrill of another visit to the Academy of Football.

This market offered a further exciting diversion in the form of a stall where I bought my first ever records. 'Speed King' by Deep Purple was one of them. I don't know why, 'cos I was never really into heavy metal. I just thought the song was alright. Then there was 'The Resurrection Shuffle' by Ashton, Gardner and Dyke – I still love that to this day – and 'Banner Man' by Blue Mink, whose singer was that black girl with big teeth, what was her name? Madeline. I think that was the other side of 'Melting Pot'.

While we're on the subject of melting pots, I'm not a Catholic – although my wife Elaine is – but there was a young priest who used to walk through the market wearing a West Ham scarf. He used to have a rabbit with everyone, he was a real character. The thing about working on markets is, even when you've had to get up at two or three in the morning at the end of a week of school with a couple of nights of boxing training thrown in, you can't help noticing people. You're in a unique position in a way. It's very much a man's world, but at the same time you're having a lot of conversations with women, because they're the ones buying your produce.

You've got to learn how to talk to people the right way, or you're never going to sell anything. So when it got towards the end of the day and I'd have to 'bang up' some cauliflowers – which basically means shouting and screaming to let everyone know you're taking the price down – the pressure would really be on. You know you've got cauliflowers left that will go pear-shaped before you get another chance to sell 'em, and no one wants a pear-shaped cauliflower, so you've got to holler, 'Come on, girls, lovely big juicy ones, two bob a time', and you've got to make it sound convincing.

If you're ever on a market and you hear people doing this, you'll probably notice the way their voice sounds, which is usually like they've just taken a deep breath, even if you know they haven't. That's because you need to puff out your chest like it's full of air as a way of showing confidence, the same way a robin does if it's having a fight in your garden.

Banging up is not an easy thing to do as a teenage boy, especially if you're at that age when you're not exactly sure which way your voice is going to go at any given moment, and you've got all these girls looking at you waiting for you to make a mistake. You know what they're like, women. 'Ooh look, he's made a mug of 'isself' – they love that 'cos it gives them one up on you. Once you know you can do it, though, it gives you confidence in other areas of your life. I suppose it's a bit like boxing in that way, or at least it was for me.

When I was fourteen, there was a girl I really fancied at school, a lovely little Jewish bird. I won't name her, because she'll know who she is and it'll be embarrassing for her, but when I found out she was doing a school play I thought, 'I'll have a go at that – get in there.' The play was *Emil and the Detectives*, and I played the newspaper boy. On paper, this was a nothing part, but it turned out to be a first step down a happy path of doing exactly what I'd normally do and calling it acting. I'm not saying I'm still on that path today, but it certainly took me a fair way in the right direction.

All I had to do was walk through the audience acting like I was selling them papers. This gave me the perfect opportunity to have a pop at the headmaster, Mr Hudson. I could dig him out by saying that he looked like Hitler dressed in his baggy suit – 'You wanna sort yourself out, son', something a bit saucy like that – and he couldn't do anything but pretend to find it as funny as everyone else did.

The whole place was laughing and I remember thinking, 'Oh, I like this.' My mum and dad came as well, and I think it was probably seeing how much I was into it that gave them the idea of me going to drama college. But I still had another year or so of banging up, doing the markets two or three times a week and generally being up and down the A10 like a whore's drawers before that would happen.

CHAPTER 11

THE BOLEYN GROUND, UPTON PARK

The first football match I went to that wasn't the 1966 World Cup was to see Southend play at Roots Hall with my uncle Len. I was always mad for West Ham – still am – but I look for Southend's results to this day, and not just because I live in Essex.

I don't have any specific recollection of the earliest times I went to Upton Park (or the Boleyn Ground in Upton Park, as it's officially called). I suppose it's like with a car or train journey that you've done your whole life – all the repetitions blur the edges of the pathway to the memory in your brain. I used to love the atmosphere of the night games, though. There was always a real buzz about the place. And the time I started going regularly, or at least to every other home game, was when me and my mate Billy Brown would take turns on the Saturday afternoons we worked at Chrisp Street Market.

It was only a bus-ride up the road, and I'd sit on the step on the side of the South Bank. Sometimes if it was quiet our dads would let me and Billy go together, and later on I started going with my mate Tony Yeates from boxing. But I never minded going on my own either. I've always been a bit of a loner, and you were part of a big crowd, anyway.

There was much more of a fun atmosphere at the Boleyn Ground in the early seventies than you get today. I find football fans in general nowadays are much more cynical and angry than they used to be. I don't know why, but I presume it's something to do with the Premier League, because it's only happened over the last twenty years or so. West Ham used to get beat a lot in the past as well, but then some of the abuse you'd hear them getting would make you laugh, whereas now there's a rage in it that makes you catch your breath.

I remember when Alan Curbishley was manager a few years back. He'd been a great player for us, and was a West Ham boy through and through. He comes from a big Canning Town family and his brother Bill was manager of The Who and producer of *Quadrophenia*. There was no reason for people not to like him. OK, Alan had been at Charlton before, but that's not exactly the crime of the century and he'd done a good job there. And yet the coating he'd get off the crowd used to stop you in your tracks. I remember thinking, 'Fucking hell! That's a bit strong', and it wasn't just me. It got to a point where one guy was giving him so much abuse that all his mates had to tell him to sit down and shut his fucking noise.

You never really got that at football years ago. People would make the odd funny remark and everyone would be laughing, and then you'd get all the firms having little rows, but that would be it. Maybe it's stopping the violence at football that's made it more miserable, because the anger's got to come out somehow.

Even though I was going to Upton Park regularly throughout the seventies and eighties – what you'd probably consider the 'golden age' of football violence, if football violence could have a golden age – the hooligans and all that never really interested me. I suppose the ideal thing would've been the Inter City Firm (ICF), but I didn't know anyone who was in it because I didn't live round there any more – a lot of them were Canning Town boys too – and I don't think I'd have been involved, anyway. I had too many other things I wanted to do.

The funny thing is, I do know a couple of those old ICFers now. They're wealthy businessmen, because they got in on the rave scene in the early days and made a lot of money. I think they're mostly in clothing these days, so at least something good came out of it all in terms of economic benefits for the area, and there's no denying they were a proper firm in their prime – better than Tottenham, anyway.

The main thing about football violence is that it's very territorial, and I never really saw things that way. Maybe if we'd stayed in Plaistow it might've been different, but by the time I was in my early teens I was so used to bombing around London on trains or Red Bus Rovers that the idea of defending one bit of turf against another didn't really make much sense to me. I was never really one for being part of a gang, either in or out of school. Obviously there were gangs about, but I tended to knock about with two or three geezers, and if we were going somewhere, it was usually because we knew someone, so I never remember thinking we'd better watch ourselves in this place or that place, because there might be trouble (except in South London, obviously).

I suppose in a way – although I never saw it like that at the time – my parents did me a favour by moving us out to Enfield, because that stopped me putting my roots down so deep in one part of East London that I couldn't go anywhere else. Me and my mates didn't really have any boundaries we wouldn't cross over. It was never like that with us. We weren't really affiliated with anyone except each other, so we were at liberty to come and go as we pleased.

Tony Yeates was a good example of how freely we moved around, because when I first met him he was boxing for the Fitzroy Lodge club in South London, but then he moved over to the Repton because that was the place to be. He's going to be cropping up a lot in this book from now on, because he's one of my best mates. In day-to-day life I usually call him Yeatesie, but that looks a bit pony written down – if he was Yates instead of Yeates it would look better – so in print I'm going to refer to him by his full name for the purpose of guaranteeing him literary immortality.

Anyway, Tony Yeates came from Bow Common, which is between Bow and Poplar. They had a famous battle there once where a firm came out of the station carrying pick-axe handles and a load of Old Bill were waiting there with shooters – I think it was one of the first few times police had been armed like that on the British mainland. They shot one of the guys in the head and the bullet went between his skull and his skin and came out the back. It was all kept very quiet at the time. The official line was that the robbers had the guns, but I've spoken to people who were there and that's not how it went down.

Obviously, none of this had anything to do with Tony, who was every bit as squeaky clean as I was. One of the great things about boxing was that it didn't just give you a legitimate outlet for any tendency towards physical aggression which might have got you into trouble otherwise, it also gave you discipline, which stopped you doing the things that make teenage kids more likely to get into strife, like taking drugs or drinking heavily before you're old enough.

Tony and I made up for lost time later of course, but when we were in our mid-teens we were too dedicated to our training to be falling over drunk or getting into fights outside the minicab office like a lot of the kids we knew from school would've been. Even a few years later when the boxing had dropped off a bit and the lure of other distractions had begun to get a bit more powerful, we'd still meet up at West Ham gym for an hour before going out for a drink.

Looking after yourself is a habit that's hard to break, and so is getting out and about. Boxing meant we had mates from all over the East End. A lot of people have their one precise patch they'll hang around in – whether that be their street, their estate, or just a particular area or neighbourhood – but we used to go everywhere. West Ham, Stratford, Bethnal Green, Hackney; it was all the same to us. We'd even go somewhere like the Isle of Dogs (which should in theory have been totally off our plot, because it was Millwall) to see my mates Billy Jobling or Russell True.

Once we'd got a bit older, in our late teens, and were young men knocking about having a drink, Moro's and the Two Puddings in Stratford and the Charleston out towards Maryland Point would become our main haunts. But sometimes we'd go further afield – even as far east as Southend or Canvey Island – to nick a bird. I know this sounds ridiculous, but at that age it felt like travelling the world. And once we came back to town, the whole of East London felt like home to us.

Back at school in Enfield I still wasn't one of those kids who knocks around in a gang – I don't mean big horrible gangs like the Crips or the Bloods, I just mean a big load of mates. It's not for me to say whether that's because I didn't want to be, or because there was no larger group that would have me. But even when it came to school trips, it'd usually just be me and a couple of mates hanging around together. I suppose because I was always off training and had my own mates from boxing, I must've seemed like I didn't really want to be part of the normal social life of the school.

I remember one skiing holiday, which my parents had kindly got the money together to pay for, when I looked around and saw that, well, it's a little bit unfair to say it was me and the nerds, but I can't think of another word that sums 'em up. All the kids who wanted to be off drinking and getting in trouble, which wasn't really my cup of tea yet, were back at home doing whatever it was they were doing. I suppose going somewhere with a load of teachers didn't seem cool to them any more. Luckily for me there was a rather nice girl called Suzanne who hadn't got that memo either, so she'd come on the trip too and all the real competition had stayed at home.

The whole lone-wolf thing would stay with me once I became an actor too. Obviously there are people in the business I'm mates with, but from the moment I got cast as Carlin in the TV version of *Scum* with all the Anna Scher boys ranged against me, I don't think I'd ever be thought of as being in a gang of actors. I think the reason why is that – without sounding too Californian about it – I kind of know who I am. I've never really reinvented myself, so I don't need the reassurance of a lot of other people being like me to tell me that I've made the right (or the wrong) decisions.

No disrespect to 'em, but a hell of a lot of actors choose to go down this particular career path because they don't like who they actually are. This isn't something I've deduced, it's something they've told me. I speak to many of them who feel that way. Don't get me wrong, they're nice kids, but they've got no history from before they became an actor, or if they have got history, it's not something they want to take with them. They're only interested in where they're going or where they are now, not where they started out.

Life's never been like that for me, because I'm proud of where I come from. But that doesn't mean I never want things to change. For instance, on the controversial subject of West Ham moving to the

Olympic Stadium in Stratford in 2016, a lot of people who ask me about it expect me to get really upset, but I don't think it's a shame at all. I will miss Upton Park, but it's always been hard work to get to. And if we want the club to progress, we've got to take the chance of a proper stadium with better transport links and parking facilities, as that's the only way to attract better players. On top of that, to be honest, the whole thing has probably been worth doing just for how much it's pissed Tottenham off.

Obviously, it was a bit of a touch for West Ham's owners, Sullivan and Gold, because they got the government to pay for the transformation of the Olympic stadium to stop it becoming a white elephant, and then sold off Upton Park to property developers. But that's business, and they're entitled to prosper so long as the club benefits in the long term.

The 2012 Olympics certainly changed the view from the end of Caistor Park Road, but the building of the actual stadium was a complete fucking con. I got myself in a lot of trouble at the time because I was asked to carry one of the flags round in front of the Coldstream Guards at the opening ceremony and I said no. I was gutted to have to do that, because obviously it was a huge event and it would've been great to be a part of it, but I'm a bit trappy sometimes. I get these bees in my bonnet and I have to let them buzz.

It wasn't the Olympics themselves I objected to – I really admire the athletes and the effort and dedication they put in – I just looked around at East London and thought, 'When we've built the hospitals and paid the teachers to be teachers and stopped closing all the fire-stations down, maybe then we can afford this, but at the moment it's an outrageous fucking liberty.'

The Olympic organisation isn't really about the sport, it's about the building, and when I see the people who run the Committee

– not so much Lord Coe, but he's a puppet, anyway – they look like white-collar gangsters to me. The corruption isn't just a side issue, it's at the heart of the whole enterprise. And FIFA are even worse.

They're a law unto themselves, and the government allow them to come in and basically rape the country that's hosting, then move on somewhere else four years later and leave the people who live there to clean up the mess. I went to the World Cup in South Africa in 2010 and had an amazing time (that was actually the biggest group I've ever been away in – we went forty-handed and stayed in Mauritius). But I also saw the way they built walls around the shanty towns and tried to sweep all the poverty under the carpet. I love sport as much as anyone, but to me there are things which are more important. It would've been an honour to carry the flag in front of the Coldstream Guards, who I love to pieces, but I had to say no, otherwise I'd have been a hypocrite for supporting something I didn't believe in.

I think you owe it to yourself to be true to your own moral code, however much flak it brings you. It's like with the Bet 365 adverts I do. People ask me why I do them. And I tell them: number one, it's very, very good money, and number two, it's for gambling which people have a choice about whether they do it or not. If you wanna gamble, you gamble; if you don't, you don't. I like gambling – I have a little flutter myself every now and again – so I have no qualms whatsoever about advertising it. But I'd never do a bank commercial or something for an insurance company, because that's something you're forced to do and it's a rip-off. They fucking slaughter you and I don't agree with that. No doubt there are plenty of people who'd see this completely the other way round – they'd be happy to take the banks' money, but wouldn't touch Bet 365 with a barge pole – but good for them if that's how they feel. It takes all sorts to make a world.

When it comes to West Ham leaving Upton Park behind, I say bring it on. If you look at the magnificent World Cup heroes' statue, just across the Barking Road from the Boleyn Cinema, it kind of makes sense that the team who won us those medals in 1966 should move to the stadium where Britain did so well in 2012. None of us live round that way any more – at least, no one I know does – and unless the younger generation of Bangladeshi kids who live there now are really into football, I don't see what good it does them to have a match there on Saturday afternoons when they're trying to run a business.

You do see a lot of the sari shops on Plashet Road will have saris in claret and blue at the right-hand end of the window (the one nearest the Boleyn Ground), but I'm not sure that's to support the team. I think that's more to stop a passing thug smashing their window. Now, I'm not saying I won't ever turn up to watch West Ham in a sari, because you never know where the tide of fashion is going to carry you. Obviously, David Beckham's tried it, but I did beat him to the punch by wearing one out in the Maldives years ago, although to be honest it probably looked a bit better on him than it did on me.

CHAPTER 12

VICTORIA PARK LIDO

I lost my virginity when I was fourteen years old. I was staying at Nanny Rich's in Shoeburyness and I met a girl on the beach. She must've been a raving lunatic because it was a freezing cold winter's day and she only had a bikini on.

There was no one else about. One minute I was just having a chat with her, and the next thing I knew I was in the woods by the mini-golf, losing my virginity standing up. I thought I'd done myself some damage afterwards.

I think she was eighteen, and I wasn't one of those kids who look older than they are. When I was fourteen, I looked it, maybe even younger. Bearing in mind our ages I suppose I was less a sexual partner and more a (willing) victim of abuse, but it didn't feel that way at the time, God bless her! I don't remember the girl's name – if I ever knew it – but I know her initials were 'GG', because she had them on a gold chain around her neck. Of course, I've loved the gee-gees ever since.

There'd always been girlfriends in my life, right back to when I was a little kid in Plaistow playing 'put a big bandage on the war hero' with the twins Kim and Tracy and Jeanie Green from down the end. Obviously the sexuality part of it is new from twelve or thirteen onwards, and it was different in those times – kids didn't mature as early as they do today.

Bikini-clad lunatics aside, the first port of call in the courtship process would usually be taking a bird up the pictures. The trouble was – aficionado of the big screen that I was even then – I always wanted to watch the film. If it was more a cuddle and a handful that you were after, you were better off taking them to a poxy movie you weren't interested in. It would probably be *Love Story* with Ryan O'Neal, and there's only one reason any heterosexual teenage boy would go and see that.

I'm not sure if it was *Love Story* (although the dates are about right, as I was thirteen when it came out) but I remember being sat in the cinema once with my arm round a girl and thinking my hand was on her threepenny when it was actually on her shoulder. She must have thought I was very sensitive to be paying so much attention to that particular area of her body – a shoulder massage would've been considered wildly metrosexual in Enfield in 1970.

By the time I got properly into my mid-teens, I'd probably be going out to a club once a week. I couldn't afford to do it more often than that, but it was possible to go up the Tottenham Royal and pull a bird on a fiver in those days. The bus-fare alone wouldn't be far off that now.

I still looked young, so I was always being asked my age on the door, but I overcame that obstacle with the same strategy which worked so well when it came to getting in to X-rated films. I used to say I was a jockey up at the Crews Hill country gallops at Enfield. It worked every time, probably because it had the element of surprise about it, as it didn't seem like the sort of story anyone would bother to make up. Even once I'd grown quite tall this ruse didn't stop doing the job for me. The only time I ever got turned away from anywhere was a few years later when I actually was eighteen. At that point I parked the jockey story, and they refused to believe I was old enough, even after they'd seen my driving licence. Sometimes it's easier to look like you're in the right when you're guilty than when you haven't actually done anything wrong, because that way your mind is properly focused on what you need to do, and innocence can breed complacency.

Once inside the Tottenham Royal, what we were all looking to do was get on the last-dance express. We weren't really much for dancing, we just used to chat with the birds and have a look about, then, when the night started to wind down, we'd be in like Flint.

I remember 'Love Train' by The O'Jays was a song that was very good to me. 'Slow one?', 'Alright, then', 'Where d'you live?', 'Stamford Hill', 'Sorry, wrong way'. If there was someone going back towards Enfield, that was perfecto, but you might consider the other direction if she was a really good sort. That's terrible, isn't it? But you know what boys are like . . . and girls ain't too far behind when it comes to being unmerciful.

My way around that was always to start off going for the ones where it looked like you didn't have a chance, because if that didn't work out you could always work your way down the scale a bit. At least that way the other girls would be impressed that you'd had the balls to give it a go and they might think they'd got a catch. It's no good starting at the bottom and trying to work your way up. Sometimes you'd get yourself in trouble by having three or four girls on the go at once and end up with nothing. But that would serve you right for getting too greedy, and next time you'd know that a bird in the hand is worth three in Shepherd's Bush.

A lot of people who get into acting or music do it for the girls (or the boys) they wouldn't have a shot at otherwise. I'm not being flash when I say that this was never what it was about for me. I already knew how to talk to a girl – or pull a bird, or whatever way you want to put it – so I never had that problem.

I'm not saying it was easy, because it wasn't. In fact, it was hard work. Looks weren't my forte. No girl worth having was just gonna see me on the dance floor of the Tottenham Royal and think, 'Oh, he's lovely.' We'd have to have a talk if I was going to get anywhere. That's why going to gigs never appealed to me, because the music was so loud you couldn't talk to anyone, and you (or at least I) couldn't pull a bird if she couldn't hear what you were saying. Me and Tony Yeates or whoever else it was would be more likely to give the big-band night at the Southgate Royalty a try, which was like a throwback to the forties. Or when we were a little bit older, we'd go to the Goldmine on Canvey Island, where they did all the Glenn Miller stuff.

Luckily, I was a bit of a past master at that thing where you and the girl are both looking across the room and you time it perfectly so that just as she catches your eye, you duck your head and look shy. It's the show of vulnerability that's the key. I used to practise on our dog, Brandy. Everyone loved him 'cos he had sad eyes, even though he was vicious. I used to watch him and think, 'Blindin'! That'll do it.' (Anthony Hopkins was the same; he had those big, watery puppy eyes too, especially when he was drinking.) Of course, this tactical approach – Brandy-eyes instead of beer-goggles, or maybe with a beer-goggle chaser – wouldn't always pay off, but I've got to tell you, the old 'Who, me . . . with all my hidden complexities?' routine worked ninety-nine times out of a hundred.

Apart from the Tottenham Royal, another venue with a bit of potential as far as girls were concerned was Victoria Park Lido. You didn't just go there to swim. I'd be down there all the time in the summer when I was fourteen or fifteen – in the morning in the school holidays, or later on for a bit of a lounge about if I'd done a hard morning on the market. There was nowhere better to have a laugh with the chaps or chat to some girls. There used to be a bit of peacocking going on, but I never really had the physique to be swaggering round the fucking pool with my budgie-smugglers on.

The lido's gone now – it was closed in 1986 and demolished a few years later – but Victoria Park is still one of the great parks of London. It used to be called 'The People's Park' because of its strong tradition of political protest, and even though it's not so much talked about as the more well-connected green spaces of West London, the avenues are so grand you could be in Regent's Park, and the boating lake's like the Serpentine, only with fewer tourists.

Everywhere else around it got bombed really badly in the war, but Victoria Park stayed pretty much intact – either because a load of ack-ack batteries were stationed there, or because the Germans wanted to keep it nice just in case they won. The feel of the place goes further back than that, though, at least it does to me. It's a real bit of old London whose bandstands and deer-park reek of the age of Empire (although the deer themselves have their own distinctive aroma).

Part of the reason I associate Victoria Park so strongly with military conquests gone by is the stories my uncle Flabby used to tell me when I'd visit him as a younger kid. Old Flabs wasn't a blood relative – I think my dad had gone out with his daughter before he met my mum – but I used to love going round to his house and listening to his tall tales of when he was in India with the British Army back in the day.

He told me some terrible stories – which are always the kind you're most interested when you're little – about how all the British soldiers in India were given an order that if they were ever in a car accident with a local they had to back up and run them over again to save on the insurance payouts. How true that is I don't know, and the same goes for the story about soldiers going over ravines on trains and deliberately pushing people off the bridges with their boots, but knowing people's inhumanity to people in occupation or wartime situations, they both kind of read as true. And maybe they give you a bit of the historical backdrop to some of the tensions between people of white and Asian backgrounds in the East End in recent years.

Apart from Britain's imperial past, the other thing Victoria Park always made me think of was armed robbery. And not just because of the time some blaggers stole my dad's black Ford Zephyr and drove it into the pond – hardly the best way to avoid drawing attention to yourself. There used to be a lot of talk locally about how many bank robbers used to train in the park. They'd jog around it planning their next blag secure in the knowledge that they were out of the range of flapping ears.

The thing about armed robbers is they're not always the fittest, but they do have that competitive instinct, so every now and then one of them would get a bit carried away with the old running and just keel over – heart attack. Maybe it's true what they say: it's a dangerous life being a blagger, but even more so if you throw a bit of jogging in as well.

Then again, there are a lot of myths surrounding those people. One of them is the idea that they always drive Jags. In fact that's the worst car to use in a bank robbery, because they've got a special switch-off button which kills the engine if you hit a kerb or something. The button is down by your right foot apparently, but you don't really want to be scrabbling around down there to restart the engine if you've gone over a level crossing too fast with the Flying

Squad on your tail. 'No Jags in blags' – that's probably the best way to remember this.

I was always fascinated by stories about the old-school London underworld. I'm not saying I was old before my years, because I wasn't. I was basically a little kid inside for a long time, probably till I was about forty (and Elaine might question whether my passport was properly stamped for the land of adulthood even then). But working on the markets and training and fighting at the Repton gave me a sense of myself as someone who could be accepted in grown-up situations from quite an early age. I was always comfortable in the company of people from older generations – whether it was my nan and granddad, or Uncle Flabs, or even the actors whose films I loved the best, who often tended to be men from earlier times like Jimmy Cagney, James Stewart or John Wayne.

There was something about those three where their flaws were also their strengths. Like in that John Wayne film where he's a bigot who hates Indians because they raped his niece – *The Searchers* – for someone like him to do a film like that was quite shocking. And obviously it's a bit later – I was doing the first *Scum* by then – but John Wayne gives an amazing performance in his last film, *The Shootist*, where he's dying of cancer and he knows it. He's just so naked and open about what his illness is doing to him, and he's not usually an actor you think of as making himself vulnerable.

Alan Hewitt was still sneaking us into the Florida in Tottenham to see X-rated films throughout my early teenage years. I remember seeing a great Italian B-movie there – probably with *Frankenstein* (the film: I wasn't dating the monster) – called *Four Flies on Grey Velvet*, where the last thing the murderer saw was these four flies on a swinging pendant. I think it's the only film I've ever seen that starts with a drum solo.

The idea that I might end up being an actor myself in films of that quality or even higher one day still wouldn't have occurred to me. Even once my mum and dad came up with the idea of me going to drama college, it wasn't something that really connected in my mind with what happened up on the big screen – I just thought of it as something to do.

What with boxing, early-morning starts for the markets, and the girls of the Tottenham Royal and the Victoria Park Lido all competing for my attention, it was no wonder there wasn't much time left for homework. Getting up for school in the morning had already begun to feel like a waste of energy that would be better put to other uses. When you meet the careers adviser and they ask what you want to do, and you say, 'I'm thinking of going to drama college', and they laugh in your face, that does give you a bit of extra motivation. You might not know exactly what your long-term goal is, but you know it's not to sit behind a fucking desk trying to crush kids' dreams.

I held the record for the highest number of detentions at Edmonton County. Detention was a pointless punishment by my way of thinking – I'd choose the cane over detention any day, and did so on a number of occasions. As far as me and school were concerned, the straw that broke the camel's back (or in this case the three-year-old thoroughbred's back) was when my dad took me off for the day to the 1972 Derby to help him sell a load of umbrellas. When the teacher asked where I'd been afterwards I was honest about it, and we got in trouble for telling the truth. My dad explained that he'd thought going to the Derby would be an education for me, but they didn't like that, so they suspended me, and I never really went back.

Whether it actually was an education is debatable – he probably just wanted somebody to carry his umbrellas for him – but it was certainly a blinding day out. At first it looked like we were on a hiding to nothing because it was a lovely sunny morning, but then it pissed down in the early afternoon and so we sold all the brollies. But that was where my dad's luck ran out, as the horse he'd put a nice few quid on in the big one that day got pushed out wide coming round Tattenham corner and Piggott said, 'See you later' on Roberto, timing his run like the master he was.

We still had a great day, though. Granddad got us into Tattersalls and Lester came walking really close to us through the enclosure. It was funny with Piggott – he was the king of Epsom, but people took the mick out of him a bit as well. He was much taller than normal for a jockey, which was why they called him 'The Long Fellow'. The two things everyone knows about him are that he was famous for his love of a pound note, and he talked the way he talked because he was deaf. Someone in the crowd put those two facts together by shouting out, 'Oi! You dropped a tenner, Lester', as he walked past us. Of course the great man turned round to pick it up, and my granddad said, 'Well, he heard that.'

When the school suspended me for taking one day off I just thought, 'Fuck 'em, I don't really need this. I'm not the brightest of sparks and I could probably stay here for the rest of my life without becoming an intellectual, so I might as well go out into the world and find something I can do that's actually going to benefit me.' It wasn't like I was a problem kid – I was doing well with the boxing, and I was always up to something. Maybe that was part of it. My mum and dad saw me in that school play and thought acting might be a way of occupying my mind and keeping me out of trouble.

I know how strange the idea of my parents sending me to a £900-a-term drama college will probably seem, because I still can't believe it happened, and I was there. Money was less tight than it had been by then, but we weren't rolling in it on any level. Maybe it was a bit of Nanny Rich's speculate-to-accumulate mentality coming in – and maybe a bit of her money as well. Or maybe that was just what was going on in my head, and my mum and dad had a different agenda. For all I know, they might've thought I was gay and the boxing was just a cover, so they wanted to get me doing some fencing and ballet to help me find myself.

Either way, at the time I don't remember thinking my dad in particular thought I was ever going to amount to anything very much, but the fact that he and my mum enrolled me in drama college says differently. OK, the Corona Academy in Ravenscourt Park didn't have that great a reputation. It wasn't exactly RADA – although ex-students did include Dennis Waterman – so you didn't really have to do too much to get in: a willingness to keep stumping up that £900 was all it took. But thinking about it now, I can see that my parents were backing me to do something different. And I owe them a lot for having that confidence in me when I might not have had it in myself.

In the long gap between me leaving school prematurely at fifteen and starting at Corona in 1973, they even got a nice Scottish drama teacher to give me some elocution lessons. Mrs McNair's daughter went to my school – I'd done an amateur play in Enfield with her – and she was a really good teacher who helped me build up confidence in my voice before I went to drama school. It was all about being able to speak clearly and with crisp enunciation – qualities for which I am now of course renowned throughout the world (and you should've heard me before I had the elocution lessons!)

CHAPTER 13

THE THEATRE ROYAL, STRATFORD EAST

When I'd left school it had been very much in a fuck-you-I'm-off kind of way, but that probably made starting at Corona more daunting, not less. It felt like a very grown-up place, more of a college than a school. I was walking into this different world without having really done anything to earn the right to be there. It's not like I'd won a scholarship for acting or gone through a gruelling audition process. My mum and dad applied on my behalf and all they had to do for me to get in was come up with £900 three times a year.

I was probably a bit embarrassed about that. I knew I was now growing up to a point where I was going to have to take responsibility for how I was living, and I couldn't rely on my mum and dad to look after me for much longer. I enjoyed my day-to-day existence, but beyond the odd little scam here and there, taking a bird out and saving up for a nice holiday every now and then, I didn't have much idea of what I wanted to do with my life.

None of the experience I'd gained being out in the big wide world – either boxing or working for my dad – seemed to count for very much at Corona. It couldn't have been much further off my usual manor without me needing a passport to get there. I had to catch the train from Lower Edmonton, change at Seven Sisters onto the Victoria Line tube to Victoria and then get the district line to Ravenscourt Park. That was a funny old journey. It took at least an hour even on a good day. On the upside, John Le Mesurier did get on my train once. I still love *Dad's Army* now, but it was a huge show then. He boarded a carriage full of schoolkids and signed autographs for all of them – what a lovely man!

There were other compensations to hold on to in my first few weeks at Corona. All the girls were beautiful and there were probably three other boys in my class who were straight, so I had a field day in that department – it was a bit of a fox-in-the-chicken-coop situation. I also had two really good teachers, Bill Happer and Vernon Morris, who both did their best to encourage me even when I was refusing to play the game.

Vernon Morris was a very good actor in his own right. He'd played the Polish traitor – the one who ends up getting hanged – in *Colditz*. What he did for me was help me get over any problem I might otherwise have had with three quarters of the geezers in the class being gay. His methods were unconventional but effective. First he sat me next to a guy called Paul, who as a child actor had been the kid who offers a cigarette to the parachuted airman in the *Battle of Britain* film, but was now the same age as me and as gay as they come.

I didn't know this at the time, but Mr Morris had told Paul to put his hand on my leg. Now, I'd never been approached like that before, and being a bit of a chap it wasn't really what I was expecting, so I just went really cold on him and said, 'Get your fucking hand off my leg!' At that point I looked up to see the whole class starting to laugh and I realised Mr Morris had set me up. 'That's what it's all about, Raymond,' he said. 'Welcome to the world of theatre.' I knew he'd done it to put me in my place a little bit, and his strategy worked. Mainly because it was for my own benefit – it wasn't like a drama-school version of *Scum* where Mr Morris was trying to break my spirit so I would succumb to the power of musical theatre.

It was actually good for me to have to find a way of fitting into a community of people from different backgrounds, either socially or in other ways, because small-mindedness was only going to hold me back in anything I wanted to do in the future. It's fear that makes you react like that. You're feeling a bit like a fish out of water, anyway, and you try to hide your anxiety about what people might say or think about you by being aggressive or abrupt or a bit of a rebel.

From that point onwards I learnt very quickly that there was no reason for me to be threatened by other people's sexuality. Anything that they wanted to get up to was their own business, and the more of them that were gay, the more girls that left me to choose from. Besides, once I got to know these kids, I found that I actually liked them – even the really posh ones, who I might have considered to be the enemy before. OK, they didn't come from where I came from, but that didn't have to be a bad thing. And if they were willing to tolerate how different my outlook on life was to theirs, then why shouldn't I extend the same courtesy to them?

That's not to say I went along with everything I was asked to do at Corona, because some of it was a bit ridiculous, but I enjoyed going there because every day was a party. And my role in the class I was in was to be the token rebellious working-class kid, so the least I could do was to act up to it.

Ballet was one of the big problem areas. I know this will come as a big surprise to all those expecting me to have a natural gift for the old *pas de deux*, but I lasted about two minutes. I dance like a boxer, anyway, and my insistence that I was going to wear Dr Marten's boots with all the ballet gear probably didn't help. I could be really fucking stubborn – and probably a major pain in the arse – when I wanted to be at that age. (Don't ask my Elaine how much I've changed since.) So everybody else probably breathed a sigh of relief when I decided to skip the ballet lessons and go to the cinema instead. I probably learnt more from the ABC just down the road from Ravenscourt Park, anyway.

Fencing classes didn't go too smoothly either. It wasn't the shouting things in French that I had a problem with – I was fine with all that '*en garde*', '*prêt*' and '*allez*' stuff – it was just a few of the finer points of the etiquette that I struggled to grasp. They had a little demonstration and I thought, 'OK, I can do that.' At first I shaped up like a fighter, but the sword is in the other hand, so you've got to go southpaw because that's the more natural way to go. Next thing I knew, there was a kid coming up to me giving it all that with the swish, swish, swish.

We squared up to each other and then instinct took over. Even years later I still can't believe I did this, but I stepped to one side and clumped him with the cup of the sword handle. At that point he's gone on the penny and while he's down on the ground I've stabbed him a couple of times just to be sure. Obviously I've not really stabbed him because the end of the blade is covered and he's got the wire mask on, but I thought that was what sword-fighting was all about. All the other kids are laughing and the instructor's going, 'No, no, no, that's not how you do it.'

The first few times you get given scripts that you have to learn is even more nerve-racking. Everyone has to work out their own way of doing it. At first I just used to read them over and over, but that wasn't really doing the job, so then I started to write them out. I would read the line and then write it out again for myself – no punctuation, just how I thought the character would say it – and that way I'd find I could really take the words in. I don't have to do that all the time now, but I still will if I've got something really heavy to learn. Generally, the better the script is, the easier it is to get the hang of it. If it's shit you'll just find yourself looking at the page thinking, 'I've got to do something to try and make this better.'

The first play I was in at drama school was called *The Trojan Women*. I'm not sure who it was by – I couldn't even pronounce the name – but I had to wear a little skinny loincloth with nothing covering my chest, and this Greek helmet with all these feathers in it. I've got the spear, the sword, everything – its almost like 'they're taking the piss, now'. As soon as I opened my mouth in that outfit everything I said sounded ridiculously London-y. It turned the whole thing into a comedy, but not necessarily in a good way – it's not a good feeling when you can see everyone laughing but you're not sure if they're laughing with you or at you.

It wasn't the most sympathetic piece of casting – I felt like a total dick. I suppose they just threw me in there thinking they'd test me, and I failed the test miserably. The next play we did was some jolly-hockey-sticks Agatha Christie thing, where I was meant to come through some French doors but one of my mates had tied them together, so I tried to squeeze in through the French windows instead and got stuck. Even though no one was taking the whole thing very seriously, once I finally got onstage it actually felt OK. I couldn't be getting any worse because the only way to go from *The Trojan Women* was up, and at least I wasn't wearing a loincloth.

The third part was the breakthrough. It was in Edward Albee's *The Zoo Story*, which I actually managed to learn properly because it was good and I wanted to do it. The play's about a couple of guys who meet on a bench in Central Park, and Mr Morris directed me and a guy called David Morris (no relation to Vernon) in it. That was where I really started to learn, partly because it was a two-hander and I like small company, and partly because I played the weaker character. I didn't have to be the nutter. I got to play the guy who was scared and had an emotional crisis. This was the first time I'd ever done anything like that, and I was surprised at how comfortable it felt – almost like freeing myself.

I enjoyed the intensity of just having two people in a scene and what happened when they met shaping the direction of the story. David Morris was a terrific actor, far in front of where I or probably anyone else was at that school at the time. With him leading the way I was improving from rehearsal to rehearsal. And by the time we finally put the play on, the audience were quite shocked by how good it was (especially given what a disaster my earlier appearances onstage had been). I could feel myself holding their attention, and when you do that it's like finding your timing as a boxer – you feint and you pull them in, then you jab and get 'em off balance. That was when I started to think, 'Maybe I can do this after all.' It wasn't just that I was taking it seriously, I was really enjoying it.

Needless to say, not every assignment at Corona went so smoothly. Shakespeare was something I thought I'd never be able to do, because it was too wordy for me and I didn't have the necessary command of the English language. As it turned out, not having that received pronunciation they teach you gave me quite a natural way of reading Shakespeare.

I did the thing I normally do, anyway, which is leave all the punctuation out. People stop in the middle of sentences all the time when they're talking, so why shouldn't characters in his plays do that too?

This technique stood me in good stead, and even though I might not have known what all the individual words meant, I seemed to be able to get across the overall meaning pretty well.

We'd have lessons on it where they'd tell us precisely what everything was supposed to mean according to the experts, but my attitude to the Shakespeare scholars was that they could fuck off. It's the same with a play as it is with a book – fair enough, the authors' intentions were important to them at the time, but it's how the whole thing comes alive in your imagination that matters to you.

Sadly, the examiners of my London Academy of Dramatic Arts exam didn't feel the same way. I'm not sure how much use those exams are – they certainly aren't going to get you a job – and they're normally incredibly boring because everyone has to do the same fucking speech. In my case it was the 'Wherefore rejoice what conquest brings' bit from *Julius Caesar*, which I probably know better now than I did then. I decided to make my version a little bit different to liven things up, so I set it in a pub. This was before Steven Berkoff and all that, so it was still quite an original idea (or at least I thought I was).

To me, the way the speech read was that this was a geezer praising the new guy coming in and mugging the old one off – the gangster who used to run that plot has been topped and all his mates are saying, 'Hold up, better get in with Tiberius.' So that's how I did it. I got zero for acting ability, which I can't argue with because it's an opinion. But the one that really got me was zero for imagination. I thought, 'Everyone else has done it exactly the same way except me, so surely I brought something to the table that no one else did?' I wasn't thinking I should've automatically got ten, but I should've certainly got something.

The good thing was that instead of discouraging me the way that it might have, the unfairness of this was actually a bit of a turning point for me. It brought my stubbornness into play by making me think, 'You're having a pop here, and I think I'm right, so I'm going to show you.' I wish I thought someone who wanted the best for me came up with this idea as a deliberate plan to motivate me, but I don't.

One of my first professional engagements was at the Theatre Royal, Stratford East. It was a revival of the Alan Klein musical *What a Crazy World We're Living In*, which Joe Brown had done as a film years before. By the time I got there in the mid-seventies Joan Littlewood (whose name was always associated with that theatre) wasn't so involved with the place any more. Her partner Gerry Raffles, who still ran it, was about to die of diabetes. He'd stood in front of the bulldozers when the Stratford shopping centre re-development threatened the theatre building with demolition, but he'd taken his eye off the ball a bit afterwards. I'd never have got cast in a role that required singing and dancing otherwise. It wasn't a very good part, and I wasn't very good in it. 'Dad's gone down the dog track/Mother's playing bingo' is one of the only lines I can remember.

I went to Stratford East with very little idea about the technique of being onstage and all that palaver, but what I learnt there about the reality of life in a professional theatre had much more impact on me than any acting tips I picked up. It turned out that my idea of it was much cleaner and more glamorous than the way things actually went down.

I'd expected almost regimental discipline and a dedication to the craft worthy of Sir Laurence Olivier. Instead, I found a load of fucking hippies smoking fags and drinking beer. I hated all the mess backstage and the whole thing felt a bit studenty for my tastes – it crushed a lot of my illusions about how the acting game was run. Maybe that was no bad thing in the long term, but when you see some actor you know off the telly and they're just like some scunger, you end up thinking, 'I don't wanna be that.' It destroys the fantasy.

As if getting paid £30 a week and a bowl of rice wasn't bad enough, you had to put up with Vanessa Redgrave coming down to tell you how you should give half your wages to the Workers' Revolutionary Party. Now I respect anybody else's opinion, but I've never been into all that commie lark. My thing was always 'you've got to look after your own', which I suppose is kind of what communism is in a way, or at least how it usually seems to turn out when people try to put it into practice. Either way, I ain't giving you £15 a week of my money. 'Sell your house, darlin'', that was how I looked at it.

I didn't say that while Vanessa Redgrave was giving her talk, of course. That would've been rude. I sat and listened to her for a while and then got up quietly to make my exit. She saw me and called out, 'Where are you going?' When I politely called back, 'Thank you, but I'm leaving. I've heard enough', she seemed pretty pissed off, because she shouted, 'But you won't learn anything unless you listen', so I said, 'Well, I won't fucking learn anything from you', and off I went.

I've never met her again since. She's a fantastic actress and she's probably a nice woman as well. I'm sure she did her bit for the party, and good luck to her, but from what I can gather it came out later on that some of the people running her organisation weren't exactly whiter than white in how they conducted themselves. A lot of that kind of sleazy shit was going on in those days, and not just in the *Top of the Pops* dressing room.

There's a Pizza Express alongside the theatre now, where we played football in the builders' sand. Another shopping centre's gone up since – the much flashier Westfield, which was opened just in time for the Olympics – but the Theatre Royal looks pretty much the same as it did forty years ago. I'm not sure it's even had a coat of paint since then. It's still there in all its horrible purple glory.

I guess we're still living in a crazy world too, so no change there either. I'll never forget the opening night of that musical. My parents came down to Stratford to watch it. My dad was all suited up with a silk hankie in his jacket pocket and he had a gin and tonic in his hand. I came off stage and I'd been terrible – danced the wrong way, told jokes no one laughed at, the lot – and he just shook his head and said, 'Give it up while you're in front, son.'

CHAPTER 14

YORK HALL

I've got to tell you about the boxing match I had in Canterbury when the Repton and Fitzroy Lodge clubs went down there together. I'd been out Kent way a couple of times before as a young kid – to the hop farms. Going 'hopping' used to be a bit of a working holiday for East End families who wouldn't have had too many chances to get out of London otherwise, but that particular boxing match was more a gypsy coach-crash than a busman's holiday.

My dad's mate Terry Spinks, who'd won the Olympic gold medal, was there. I'm on the scales weighing in ready to fight. I've got the velvet shorts on, the green-and-gold top – to be honest with you I look a million dollars (if I don't say this, no one else is going to). Then the kid I'm fighting gets up there. He's got a pair of old pumps, baggy shorts, no front teeth and a broken hooter. So straight away I'm thinking, 'He's been hit a few times, this is gonna be easy.'

Right from the start of the fight, I'm just going ping! Picking him off nicely. Can't miss – he's walking into 'em. Then at the end of the first round, I hit him square on the chin and he's straight down on the canvas – wallop! He came out for the second like a fucking lunatic – bit me, elbowed me, kneed me in the groin, stood on my feet, hit me with everything. He just lost the plot completely. I probably won the fight easier than I would've done otherwise, but he did make me pay for it. I don't think I got out of bed for a day and a half afterwards.

He was a little rat, but he had some heart. My career record as an amateur boxer was eighty wins out of eighty-eight fights, and in all that time I met one opponent I disliked as a person. It wasn't this kid with the broken hooter, it was another guy who I could tell was a nasty fucker from the moment we shook hands.

Even while I was boxing him, I was thinking, 'You are not a nice fella.' He had all the technical knowledge to be a good fighter, so why was he trying to head-butt me in the clinches? He didn't want to know when it was time to shake hands after I'd beaten him, either, and I just thought, 'You can go fuck yourself. You've just had one hiding – do you want another one?'

That fight was one of the very few bad memories I took away from York Hall in Bethnal Green. Obviously there's Wembley and the Albert Hall as well, but as far as grassroots boxing in England goes, York Hall is the home of it. The building is a swimming pool in the daytime, so if you go there at any other time, it doesn't really feel like anything special. But I had some great nights there, and when you step into that ring and the roar goes up, there's an atmosphere like nowhere else – because it's a municipal baths, you can imagine the echo you get.

I had thirteen wins at York Hall, and it's been my lucky number ever since.

A boxing match is nothing like street fighting. First off because you've got a referee to stop it – that's a major difference. Also, street fights (when they're not a formal 'straightener' like that time in Spitalfields Market) are usually over anger, whereas if you let anger come into boxing, you're probably going to lose.

The one time I lost at York Hall, it wasn't me who got angry. The kid I was boxing was good and it was close, but I thought I won it. In fact, it was probably the best I've ever boxed. But the Repton was a big club, and every now and then they used to surrender someone to make it look fair. York Hall was effectively our home venue so they had to show that we weren't in control of the decisions, and that night it was my turn to be sacrificed. Well, that's my story and I'm sticking to it. I know this might sound like I'm making excuses, but as a general rule in boxing you know when you've won and you know when you've lost.

Either way, old Sammy Keyworth who worked with us on Roman Road Market wasn't too happy about the decision. He'd come along to watch me fight, and when the verdict went against me he took umbrage in a major way. The mayor of Tower Hamlets was sitting in front of him, and Sammy was so angry he kicked the guy's chair over. The mayor went flying in all his regalia, chains and ermine everywhere – it was hilarious.

I got a nice little consolation prize at the end of that evening when I won the Fighter of the Night award from the Marksman pub. As you can imagine, it was pretty unusual for that to go to a boxer who'd lost, so I think that showed where their sympathies lay.

Another great night at York Hall was when I won John H. Stracey's trophy as Fighter of the Year for going a whole twelve months undefeated. He's a great mate of mine even now, John. I'll never forget the time he won the world title against José Nápoles. The funny thing about that was that they didn't televise the fight live – it wasn't on till the day after, and the commentator (I can't remember if it was Reg Gutteridge or Harry Carpenter) had to put the voiceover on afterwards, pretending he hadn't already seen it. But he couldn't help himself, so he kept saying things like, 'I definitely feel John H. Stracey is going to win.'

The East End had more than its fair share of world boxing champions in those days. Charlie Magri was another one. He was a great boy, Charlie – I think his dad was a tailor. He boxed at the Arbour youth club in Stepney, which wasn't far from the Repton, and he was about the same age as me, so we all became mates when he was coming up through the ranks. I was there when he won the world title and I had a drink with him after he lost it. You made so many connections in boxing – more than any other business I've ever come across, and they're real friendships as well. Obviously you meet a lot of people in the acting game, but there's more loyalty in boxing.

I had three fights in one night at York Hall once at the London Federation of Boys Clubs championships (which I think I'm still the only person to have won in three different years). That took me right the way through to the NABC's, but it all went wrong with the last punch of the semi-finals. I jabbed the fella and he ducked his head and took my hand under with him, which broke the finger on my jabbing hand. If it had been the right hand I'd have probably got away with it, but as it was I couldn't box in the final. Obviously, I was gutted at the time, but I'd have had to take on a good fighter. His name was George Walker, and he was a big strong kid who might have been too much of a handful for me, anyway, at the time. But we'll never know because he got a bye and became the champion.

Boxing for the Repton does open doors, because it is a big famous club and they do produce some great fighters, but I never looked at myself as being good enough to join them. That's not me being modest, I honestly didn't imagine myself as being that good at anything. I never had that . . . inner belief is, I suppose, what you call it. Even now when I watch a sportsman perform really well I always think it's absolutely fantastic, but I never see what they're doing as something I'd be capable of, any more than I did when I saw Bobby Moore lift the World Cup.

I did get to box for England a couple of times. I was still a junior then – maybe sixteen – and I got picked because I'd won the Middlesex and London championships, which automatically gives you the chance to box for your country. I'd have been a light welterweight at that time, and it was a home nations fixture, England versus Wales.

There were two bouts and I boxed a kid called Gary Ace in the first one. They're tough kids from that part of the world and he was a good fighter, but I had the secret weapon that was Repton coach Jackie Bowers in my corner. You never wanted to go back in your corner at the end of the round when Jackie was there because he'd give you a harder time than the other fighter would. He'd tell me, 'You'll never be a fighter', and I'd say, 'I don't want to be a fucking fighter, Jack – do you think I want to get punched in the face all my life?' That's how the conversations between us used to go.

I had a lot of time for Jackie, both as a coach and as a man, and he did me proud that night. Because I was known as a counter-puncher, Gary was expecting me to be on the back foot from the off so Jackie said, 'Just walk straight across and hit him on the chin with a right-hander.' I did, and he went straight through the ropes. That kind of livened him up and from that point on I boxed beautifully – he says modestly – and I won in the end. My other fight was against another little Welsh tough-nut. I did alright in that one as well, but not alright enough to win. I'm not saying I was robbed, but it was a good job Sammy Keyworth wasn't there.

Although I appreciated my dad coming to watch me, I always thought I boxed better when he wasn't there. He used to get rather excited, and I suppose I was more worried about what my dad was thinking than I was about what I was doing. I bear that in mind with my eldest girl Lois these days. She's a singer and I really like what she does, but I don't go to every gig – even though she wants me to – because I like her not to have to worry about what I'm thinking of it.

I had a particular way of being nervous before a fight, which is still how I get to this day when I'm doing a film. Some people would be physically sick with nerves, but I'd get very tired and start falling asleep instead. I'd try to keep myself going but I'd just feel really lethargic – I think it was the loss of all the energy my nerves were burning. I'd get a kind of fear as well. Not a fear of being punched – well, I suppose there might have been a bit of that – but more a general anxiety about not doing what you're supposed to do, just forgetting it all. That's how I'd feel until the bell went at the start of the first round, then I'd wake up – like the drunk guy in the pub who springs to attention when he hears 'last orders'.

I'm more or less the same on a film set, even now. There's always that fear in the time leading up to it. You're thinking, 'Why couldn't I have done this yesterday when I was feeling great, instead of today when I've got no energy and can't remember the words? What are the fucking words again?' Then someone shouts 'Action!' and nine times out of ten – thank God – it's alright. You work the scene out because you've got a fine actor opposite you, the timing's working and bam! some energy floods into you.

That's why I say boxing was probably more of an education for me as an actor than stage school was (apart from the ballet, obviously – that was an essential). Because without the boxing I wouldn't have known what that feeling is where you step through the ropes into the ring thinking, 'Why am I putting myself through this shit?'

Whether you're climbing into the ring or walking onstage there's no fundamental difference, what matters is what you do next.

I remember the first senior fight I had at the age of seventeen. It was at Alan Minter's club in Crawley, and I've got to tell you that when I was seventeen, you'd have looked at me and guessed I was at least fucking twelve. I was reasonably tall – five foot nine or ten – but I looked like I should still be in shorts and plastic sandals. I think I've said before that when you get in the ring you have a little look in the guy's eyes opposite and you know whether you're going to win or not. This time, when the other geezer took his gown off, he was covered in tattoos (and this was when having a tattoo still meant something) and hairy as a fucking gorilla. I don't know what they're putting in the water down Crawley way. He was meant to be my age but he looked about thirty-five.

All of a sudden you're not boxing boys any more, you're boxing men. It's like moving up from borstal into prison. I mean, the geezer had hairy legs – I'd never had a hair on my legs in my life! At this point you either decide you've got no chance and give up, or you approach it like a chess match and try to find a way to win. The first round I went with plan A and I was just totally overwhelmed. But then I went back in my corner and thought, 'Fuck this!' The second round I started boxing differently and it was much more even. Then I pissed the third round and won the fight.

That discipline of standing there thinking, 'I can't do this', and then taking a deep breath and giving it a go really stands you in good stead for the rest of your life. It's not just a matter of digging deep inside yourself, you've also got to clear your mind. The way you calm yourself down and convince yourself that nothing's impossible is almost like meditation – that's what gives you the confidence to keep yourself out of harm's way. If you do it right, you can almost get a feeling that the other geezer can't hurt you (even though obviously they can). It's funny with pain, I find I've got a way of switching it off. I don't know if that's a good thing or not, because sometimes pain is there for a reason.

It's the same with a script where there's something dark or difficult that's going to happen. You've got to close that down a bit so you can go beyond it. And the fear you have when you first pick it up and maybe think you can't do it is the thing which is going to help you do that. It's the equivalent of Jackie Bowers in my corner when I was boxing a kid called Terry Parker at the London Feds Finals. I came back at the end of the first round and got beaten up worse than I had been in the ring. Jackie's slapping me round the head going, 'C'mon, liven up', and I'm thinking, 'Fuck that, I'd rather be out there boxing than in here fighting him.'

Once you're out there, that's when the ringcraft comes in – the stuff that Billy Howick taught me at the Repton. It's all about the positioning of your feet and where you move – all the little tricks of pushing someone's arms down to get them off balance and then getting a jab in. A lot of it is kind of on the borderline of being illegal, but there are ways of being illegal which are still within the spirit of the game. And so long as the head coach Burnsy's matched you up not to get hurt, like he always does, hopefully you'll keep the old face intact.

CHAPTER 15

THE PROSPECT OF
WHITBY, WAPPING

It was partly going to Corona that pushed boxing into the wings. But the gloves were also coming off as far as drinking was concerned, and they were already long gone when it came to girls. I didn't give the boxing up for good. I would put the gloves back on and return to the ring for two more fights a couple of years later, but that would be my Elvis in Vegas phase.

In the meantime, the discipline I'd learnt at the Repton helped keep me out of some of the scrapes I'd probably have got into otherwise, but not all of them. One incident which has stuck in my mind, for reasons which will soon become obvious, was when I went away for a few days with a mate from drama college called John Walford. His mum lived with a French Basque geezer in Andorra, this strange little tax haven in the Spanish Alps who are one of the few teams England can usually be expected to beat in the World Cup.

Now, the Spanish and the French Basques don't tend to get on with one another particularly well, but I wasn't too bothered about all that. I was too busy sliding around the place in all this moody ski gear – basically a pair of jeans and a woolly hat. One night we went to a club that was up on the top of this mountain. It was full of Spanish and French, not mixing particularly well. You know that feeling when you walk into a room and you can just smell the trouble that's coming? This was one of those.

The French fella we were with was some kind of karate expert, and when it all eventually went off he started really putting himself about, karate-chopping everyone. If I'd had a choice I probably wouldn't have been on his side, but I didn't have a choice because all these Spanish geezers attacked us. In that kind of mass tear-up you basically just end up hitting anyone who's near you who you didn't come in with. We're dishing out a few good clumps, but we're taking some as well.

What you don't want in that situation is for someone to take things up a level, and John's mum's boyfriend pulling out a gas gun and shooting the geezer next to him in the chest with a flare was never really going to calm things down too much. The other guy went up like a human torch. Although he was alright in the end because everyone jumped on him to put the fire out, I had to get John's mum and throw her under the table to keep her out of the free-for-all that followed. At this point, the Old Bill – or the Vieux Guillaume as the French call them – arrived, and whatever language we were speaking, this was definitely a 'stoppo'.

We all sprinted out the side door, Johnny's mum and the French fella jumped in one car, and me and Johnny got in his little motor which we'd been running around in, and now we're bombing down the mountain. It's about one o'clock in the morning and we're both quite bruised up after taking a few good clumps (as well as having had a fair bit to drink). John sees a bend coming up and puts his foot down hard on the brake – never the best idea when you're driving on black ice. As the car starts to spin, I'm looking out of the window and it's a good thousand feet down the side of the mountain. I'm not exaggerating – the Pyrenees are high. I'm thinking, 'This is it, I'm gonna die.'

The car spun and it spun and all I could see was down. There was no panic – just a total feeling of calm and knowing there was nothing we could do about it. Then we smashed into a wall and came to a dead stop. It was a bit too much like the end of *The Italian Job* for comfort.

We sat there for a minute in silence, probably shaking a bit and just getting used to the fact that we were still alive. Then we started to think, 'What are we gonna do now?' The car was a write-off and no one who came past seemed that into stopping, so we had no choice but to walk down the mountain. It took us about an hour, and when we finally got to the town we went into this little place and ordered some strawberries and cream and a bottle of champagne. It was almost like 'this is the first day of the rest of the life which just nearly ended'.

Brushes with death notwithstanding, I was primed for going abroad by then. I love going to places I've never been to before, and the great thing about the kind of travelling I do now in the film industry is that you don't necessarily go to the same places as normal tourists do. You'll end up in the parts of a country where people actually live. I suppose my lucky escape in Andorra was a foretaste of things to come in that area. These days I try to get into and out of a place without participating in a mass brawl like you'd get in an old-fashioned Western, although I was fine with that back then. I didn't know who or what I was meant to be fighting for, I was just hitting everybody who came near me. I was a mercenary doing it for love – Margaret Thatcher's son Mark had nothing on me.

John Walford changed his surname to Segal later on and became quite a successful actor for a while. There was a David Niven-ish quality about him that the birds liked (and he liked them back), almost a gentleman-fraudster kind of thing. His mum was a survivor as well. She was still a good-looking woman and it turned out she knew the chief of police in the town, so the whole flare-gun thing got nicely smoothed over and I managed to get home to Blighty without having to bring the consulate into it.

Obviously not everyone who went to Corona got the chance to have a career as a professional actor when they left – in fact, if you did you were kind of the exception that proved the rule. Even my old *Zoo Story* sparring partner David Morris never really got a break, which was a shame because he was good enough to make it – he really was.

What tended to happen was that you might get a few little chances as an extra or in small speaking parts and whether or not anything came of it was kind of in the lap of the gods. I could tell you that I was grateful for any opportunities that came my way and did my best to grasp them with both hands in an appropriately appreciative and professional manner, but that would be a complete load of bollocks.

Truth be told, I was a bit of a handful at this stage in my life. I'd found it quite easy to adjust to the kind of discipline boxing required, but knowing how to behave at casting calls was a completely different matter. I wasn't used to people treating me like a piece of shit in normal life, and I wasn't ambitious enough to accept it in the interests of getting a part.

The first audition I ever turned up for was in Reading, and I was late 'cos I had to get the train and I didn't really know what I was doing. It was for something called *The Perils of Pauline*. I'm not sure if it ever even came out because the most recent film with that title which I could find on the internet was made in America in 1967. Anyway, I finally got in there and the casting woman really had the hump. I said, 'I'm really sorry, I got lost. I've never done this before.' She was really short with me and just sort of hissed at me, 'Sit down, you're not in this scene.'

I remember thinking, 'I ain't gonna like this much if that's the way they're gonna talk to me.' But the scene they were filming at the time was some kind of basketball game, and at that point someone blew a whistle and all the girls took their tops off. Turned out it was one of those things they made a lot of in the mid-seventies that are a bit raunchy but not quite raunchy enough to be soft porn. Either way, there were threepennies everywhere, and even though I didn't get the part, I did get the train back to London thinking, 'Maybe there's something to this acting game after all.'

Not long afterwards, I went up for a part in the Ken Russell film *Lisztomania*. We all had to stand in a row and this woman with blue hair came down the line with the great man. It was for a little Hitler scene where you had to have your hair cut like *der Führer* (Adolf, not Ken), so she was going down the line kind of barking at us: 'You, get your hair cut. You, get your hair cut . . .' She wasn't even looking at us properly as she was saying it, and it seemed like she was channelling the spirit of the Nazis a little bit too effectively.

So when she got to me, I just told her: 'I don't want my hair cut.' When she told me I'd have to if I wanted the part, I asked her how much extra you got paid for having your hair cut and she said, 'Nothing.' Then she asked me if I even wanted to be in the film and I said, 'No, because I don't want to fucking look like you.' Part or no part, I wasn't having someone treating me so disrespectfully. And I didn't regret standing up to her, even when I found out she was Ken Russell's wife.

It would be wrong to characterise this as an isolated incident. There was another time when I got sent up for some work as an extra in *Get Some In*. It was an ITV sitcom about National Service which my mate Karl Howman – who I'm going to tell you about in a minute – ended up starring in. He hadn't got there yet, though; I think Robert Lindsay was doing it at the time, maybe before he did *Citizen Smith*. Anyway, all of us extras were standing there in our RAF bits while the actors did their piece. And instead of just asking me to move, the director kind of picked me up and moved me by my shoulder.

I was a skinny little thing in those days, so he probably thought it would be OK. But it wasn't, because I turned round and nutted him. He went sprawling over the chairs and I was obviously asked to leave the premises in no uncertain terms. At that point I was looking around to see if anyone else wanted to have a fight, but no one did, so I was out of there.

After that, Corona became a bit reticent to send me up for things, which I suppose I couldn't really blame them for, as I was a bit of a little fucker and I probably wasn't doing the school's reputation any good either. Maybe I just wasn't quite ready for the film industry, or the film industry wasn't quite ready for me. Either way, to be honest, I'm still a bit the same today. Ask me nicely and I'll do anything for you, but if you're trying to mug me off, sitting in the director's chair (or next to it) won't get you a free pass.

It wasn't that I wasn't willing to learn. I got a part-time job as the token straight man with all the lesbians and gays in the wardrobe department at the National Theatre for a while, when it was still at the Old Vic. You'd get £28 a night or something like that, which wasn't bad compared to what the Theatre Royal Stratford East was paying (and there was the added bonus that you didn't have to give any of it to Vanessa Redgrave). The three plays they were doing at the time – because they revolved them at the National even then – were *Playboy of the Western World*, *Hamlet* and another one. My job was looking after two actors called Patrick Monckton and Michael Keating, but sometimes a mate of mine (John Walford/Segal again) who was looking after Albert Finney would be off and I'd have to stand in for him.

Finney had been one of my favourite actors ever since I'd seen him in *Saturday Night, Sunday Morning*. It didn't matter that he was playing a Northerner – I recognised that character, and that was the first time I'd ever seen the kind of person I could relate to from my own life up there on the big screen in such a convincing way. I used to love watching him in *Hamlet*, giving it the full Shakespearian thing, but doing it as a man, so I'd go missing during the play to watch him from the seats right upstairs at the back.

Unfortunately I was late getting back once and Albert missed his cue. As I went running round the back to help him, Susan Fleetwood came off the stage after the mad scene. I think she'd got a bit carried away during that one because she picked up my hand and placed it firmly on her left tit saying, 'Feel my heart.' I said, 'It's not your heart I'm feeling, Susan.'

I went in the bar afterwards knowing I'd fucked up, which I felt really bad about, as I had a lot of time for Albert Finney as a person, never mind how great his acting was. I still wasn't quite ready to face the music, though, so when he came in looking for me, I ducked down behind a table. Through the forest of furniture legs I could clearly see Albert's human ones walking across the floor, so I crawled off between the stools in the opposite direction.

When I came up for air, there he was standing right in front of me, like one of the twins in *The Shining*, only with Albert Finney's face. I don't know how he did it; it was like he floated there or something. His first two words were not promising – they were 'You' and 'cunt' – but when I explained, 'Albert, I'm so sorry I fucked up, I was watching you from up the back and I just missed the call', it seemed to do the trick. All he said after that was, 'What do you want to drink?'

Even though I was only in the wardrobe department, I was quite proud of the fact that I was part of the company for the crossover from the Old Vic to the new building on the South Bank, which might have been a bit of a concrete block but it had great theatres inside it. Being out and about doing that was much better than just being stuck in Corona doing little plays. Not only did the wages help pay my tube fare into college in the mornings, I was also getting paid to watch the kind of actors I admired go to work at close quarters. It wasn't just Albert Finney, there were Angela Lansbury, Frank Finlay and Dinsdale Landen as well; all of whom were great technicians, far beyond any level that I could ever aspire to.

Not all of my early brushes with the film and TV industries were quite as disastrous as the Mrs Ken Russell and *Get Some In* incidents. Occasionally my ebullient approach to the kind of small parts I was getting offered at that time paid off. At the age of eighteen, I was cast in an episode of *The Sweeney* called 'Loving Arms'. It was meant to be a non-speaking role where I was at a table in the pub with a guy who was buying a gun, but I couldn't (or wouldn't) stop myself improvising dialogue with him.

The director kept saying, 'Excuse me, quiet, please. You're not meant to talk in this scene.' Now I didn't know they had to pay you an extra £30 for talking – that's why they want you to keep schtum – but John Thaw and Dennis Waterman obviously did, because they were standing at the bar laughing while I was arguing the toss. They weren't being horrible, they could just see how green I was. My point of view was: 'It just seems silly that I'd be sitting here not saying anything when we're doing something as important as buying a gun', but the director still insisted I keep quiet, so I ended up taking the gun off the guy and having a look at it.

The director was climbing the walls at this point, telling me to put the gun down, but I was getting pissed off now. 'Well, what do you want me to do?' I asked him, 'Just sit here and play with my cock?' I suppose it was good of him not to just send me home after that, but this was one of my first-ever paid jobs so I didn't know any better. And I got the last laugh at the end, because for the next scene we had to go out in the street where me and the guy with the gun had to run away. I was supposed to get caught, but instinct took over and I jumped over a fence and escaped. They didn't have time to reshoot the scene so it had to stay in done my way. I've seen the episode quite recently – I think it's out there on the internet somewhere – and it's quite funny. One minute I'm running alongside the other guy, the next I'm gone.

Another of my first paid outings in front of the cameras brought me into contact with someone who's still one of my best friends now. I'd got a day's work as an extra on the David Essex film *Stardust*, down by the Thames at the Prospect of Whitby pub in Wapping. It's one of the oldest – if not the oldest – riverside pubs in London, and Captain Cook lodged just around the corner for a while, so he probably would've had a drink in there at some point.

This was in 1974, so it was still all old warehouses down that way then. The cobbled streets are still the same forty years later, but all the warehouses have been turned into flats now.

Karl was in one of the bands in the film (with Keith Moon, who was his great mate at the time). I'd never met Mr Howman before, and when I got my lunch and went upstairs with it on one of the double-decker buses they do the catering on, I didn't see him sitting up the back. Then he said, 'Alright?' and asked me to join him, which was a nice thing to do because I was only an extra and he had a much bigger part. He's a South London boy, which is unusual for me in friendship terms, but I'm not prejudiced. I think his dad was a colour sergeant in the band at the Woolwich Arsenal.

Anyway, we started talking and became mates – not close mates who keep in touch and everything, but mates. Then a few years later, in the late seventies he played my brother's friend in the ITV series *Fox*, we remembered each other and it went from there. I think Karl was playing the young copper in *The Long Good Friday* around that time, and I was just about to get married. Once our wives palled up too that was it, and we've been going on holiday together with the kids ever since. We've got in a few scrapes together too, over the years, but they might have to wait for volume two.

In the meantime I'd still – as my old mate Bob Hoskins used to say – 'got overheads', and one way of dealing with them was to get a bit of work doing adverts so people could dig them up to put on TV shows and embarrass me years later. My sister Laura did a bit of modelling in her teenage years, and through her I ended up signing with a place called the Norrie Carr Agency.

It was thanks to them that I ended up doing a low-calorie bread commercial where I had a cap on and I followed the Slimcea bird down the road before she went off in a balloon. Then there was one for Pot Noodle where I had to climb up and down some ladders. As you might have noticed, it was only the most high-end products that wanted to use me.

The most painful one of all was the ad for Double Diamond pale ale (apparently it's still Prince Philip's favourite beer, which just goes to show money can't buy you good taste). It had all these old *Carry On* actors and people you knew in it – Liz Fraser, she was one of them – then at the end the camera settled on me and this other kid holding pint glasses, and the slogan said: 'And here's another two mugs you might recognise.' Not only were we nobodies, we were nobodies selling Double Diamond – we had literally mugged ourselves off.

CHAPTER 16

NASHVILLE'S, WHITECHAPEL

I was lucky to be starting out as an actor at a time when people in the TV and film industries had just about got used to the idea of casting real kids from real areas. The BBC's *Play for Today* slot had a lot to do with it – take that out of the equation and it might still all be 'Gorblimey, guv'nor, can I doff my cap for you, sir?' And you'd have probably ended up with Hugh Grant in *Sexy Beast* instead of me. His head would have wobbled a lot in that role. Especially once Gandhi got hold of him.

A few years back when I was doing a film called *Macbeth on the Estate*, I had a conversation with some of the West Indian geezers who were in it about how the black actors they saw on TV didn't seem to represent them. These kids didn't feel like they were allowed in the game. It occurred to me that they were facing exactly the same problems that white working-class actors used to have. It's probably the writers and directors who are the key: the more people who come from where you come from and know what they're talking about start to make inroads

141

into the business, the more chance you've got of telling your own stories.

By the mid-seventies, more than a decade had passed since the kitchen-sink dramas brought Richard Harris and Albert Finney and that whole generation through. When characters that you'd consider to be normal working people turned up on TV or in film roles, you didn't expect them to be some posh bloke putting on an accent any more. It was the time just before punk, and it was almost becoming fashionable to talk like me or the dowager Phyllis Daniels. What opened so many doors for us was the fact that directors like Ken Loach and Alan Clarke and Frank Roddam were starting to have enough clout to get the kind of films made that would need actors like us to be in them.

I was the token working-class kid at Corona, but there were already a couple of others there who were making themselves out to be that too (admittedly on slightly shakier credentials). The school acted as our agency, but without the kind of philanthropic intentions that guided Anna Scher. Basically it was a money-making machine, whereas Anna's was all about encouraging kids who might need a bit of help to come out of their shell. That was a fantastic thing, but I've got no regrets about not going there. I didn't know it existed at that time, anyway, and going to Corona was the kind of chapter in your life that makes you what you are. There I was a minority of one. If I'd gone to Anna Scher's, I'd have been just like everyone else.

Les Blair was another one of those directors who wanted to put actual working-class people on the screen, rather than the cardboard cut-out variety. Another of my first proper pieces of TV work was a thing for him called *Sunshine in Brixton*. It was about a school football team, and doing that was when I met all the boys from Anna Scher: Tony London, who was a really good actor and became a close mate of mine for a while, Ray Burdis and Elvis Payne among others.

I enjoyed meeting them all, but that didn't necessarily mean I wanted to join their gang. It was a funny old film, that. One of the main characters in it was this black guy with dyed blond hair who was called 'The Negative'. For me, the experience was all positives. Although this was my first time being in front of the cameras for extended periods and I could tell that I had a lot to learn, I definitely felt like I was getting somewhere.

I still have much to thank Bill Happer and Vernon Morris for, because I wouldn't have lasted nearly as long as I did at drama college without them nurturing and protecting me a little bit. I think those two must have thought I at least had something – not that they ever told me – because I was such a monumental pain in the arse at the time, why would they have bothered with me otherwise?

To say that other people in the Corona hierarchy viewed me with less enthusiasm would be putting it mildly. By the time I'd been there a couple of years, things were coming to a head. They'd fitted me up for the angry young man role and I was kind of acting up to it. I probably was a bit like that inside, anyway, but when you know that's all people are expecting of you, sometimes you mask your disappointment with an extra layer of bravado. That's probably how the *Get Some In* and *Lizstomania* incidents came about – because I felt like a fish out of water, I was more likely to behave like one.

In the autumn of 1976, which should have been the start of my last year, Corona didn't just stop sending me out for auditions, they started actively trying to keep the other kids away from me. They said it was because I was 'a bad influence, language-wise', which I can understand now, but at the time it made me feel like a nonce. I thought they were being snobby about the way I spoke, and they probably were. I don't think the big news about the increasing fashionability of working-class accents had quite got through to them yet.

Either way, at the end of that term there was a Christmas party at the college which I specifically wasn't invited to. Everyone else was, but not me. When I asked about it they didn't even have the decency to pretend my invitation got lost in the post. I was fuming, and as a result I did something really pathetic which might have been designed to confirm their worse assumptions about me. I got a lolly stick, glued some tacks on it and put it under one of the tyres on the headmistress's car.

Thinking about that now, it was fucking dangerous – she could have been on the motorway or something when the tyre went. Luckily for me, she didn't make it out of her official parking space. One of the other kids was summoned into her office and threatened with expulsion unless they turned in the culprit, so they lollied me right up – which I couldn't really blame them for, as they didn't come from where I came from – and I was expelled on the spot. To be honest, all concerned probably breathed a sigh of relief when that happened, not least my mum and dad, who wouldn't have to find the £900 a term any more.

The day I was expelled, some of the other boys were going out to audition for a BBC TV play called *Scum*. Obviously, I wasn't because I was considered too badly behaved to be trusted as an ambassador for Corona's reputation. But I went along with them, anyway, so we could all go out for a beer together afterwards to say goodbye.

I've told this story a lot of times over the years but I'm not going to add any dramatic embellishments about statues being seen crying in the foyer of the BBC or my mum making me a piece of toast for breakfast in the morning that had John Blundell's face on it. While I was waiting outside for the others to do their auditions I got talking to the receptionist, who was a lovely girl and just the sort of person any red-blooded young man would want to be whiling away the hours with. After I'd been chatting her up for a while she asked me, 'Do you wanna go in and meet the director?' I said, 'No, thanks, not really, darling – that ain't really my scene no more.'

She persisted: 'Go on, he's really nice.' So on her advice I went in and met Alan Clarke, who obviously I'd never heard of at that point, and we had a laugh together. I didn't know what the part was and I didn't really care when he said it was originally written for a Glaswegian. Alan told me afterwards that it was only because I was the last one in that he watched me walk out of the door and down the corridor afterwards. But that was why he gave me the job, because I walked down the corridor like a fighter, which of course is what I was. If that's not fate, I don't know what is. If there'd been one more person coming in after me, you wouldn't be reading this book now, and God knows what I'd be doing.

It wasn't just through divine intervention from a BBC reception-ist that the stars had aligned for me to play Carlin in *Scum*. A couple of the kind of incidents which no drama college would workshop had also helped prepare the ground. Both of them involved the iron bar we used to stop the front gate in Enfield hitting the flowers behind it being employed for another purpose.

The first time had been when I was still in my early teens. I was playing football with some of the other local kids in the alleyway that ran up the side of our house in Enfield. We used to put jumpers down to make one goal at our end of the alleyway, and a wall at the far end, which was the back of the maisonettes' garages, served as the other.

In the end house, two along from where I lived, there was a cou-ple who had a great big lump of a son. I suppose he must've been in his mid-thirties. Remember we're just kids, and we're probably making a bit of a noise, but there's no history of that being a problem. I suppose the geezer must've had a bad day or something, because instead of him just coming out and telling us to turn it down a bit, he's come running straight towards me.

In my innocence I thought he was wanting to join in the game and have a bit of a kickabout, so I dropped my shoulder to take the ball around him. The next thing I knew he'd grabbed me by the throat and slammed me up against the fence of the cemetery we used to play about in trying to scare people.

At this moment, it just so happens that my dad is looking out of the window and sees what's going on. So he appears from nowhere, grabs the iron bar from behind the front gate and, in a single graceful movement, vaults over the wall. He's got this move down to a tee. You'd think he'd practised it (and who knows, perhaps he had done). Either way, he runs up to the guy who's got me by the throat and tells him to put me down.

Now this geezer is a big unit and for whatever reason he's pretty angry, so as he puts me down he steps towards my dad, which is a big mistake. Because my dad leaps up in the air and hits him straight across the top of the head with the iron bar. He could've killed him, and to be honest at that moment I think he might've meant to, because he'd seen what the guy was doing to me, and my dad's instinct to protect his family was very strong.

I'll never forget what happened in the next few seconds. The fella did the splits as the weight of the bar forced him to the ground. Then he was instantly, violently sick from the clump on the head, before going out like a light – sparko – on the pavement. It scared the life out of me, but the additional anxiety that my dad might go to prison for what he'd just done didn't come to me till a bit later on.

It didn't seem to bother my dad, though. He just turned round, put the iron bar back in the flowerbed, and went back to whatever he was doing. I'd like to say that we went back to our game of football as well, but of course we didn't. And not long after we'd all melted away a bit lively an ambulance came, and my dad was charged with causing grievous bodily harm. He was lucky they didn't try to do him for attempted murder, to be honest.

We always say don't get the police involved, but if someone else does and you've got an out, then it's best to counter-nick 'em. This was a lesson that would come in handy for me later in life, and it was exactly what my dad did – he counter-nicked the other guy for assaulting me. Not only was this an effective tactic, it was also fair enough, because the geezer did have me round the Gregory, and I was only a kid. In the end they both went to court, although I don't remember having to give evidence, and the judge bound the two of them over to keep the peace for a year.

They managed it for longer than that, because we never saw the other guy again. Apparently he did recover from the attack physically, but if he ever came round to see his mum and dad after that, he did so at night. Even I'm a bit shocked by how brutal that looks written down, but in this book violent incidents are like London buses – you wait sixteen chapters for them and then two come along at once.

The iron bar's second appearance was on the night of the ABA finals. These always used to take place on the eve of the Cup Final at the old Empire Pool, Wembley (now spruced up a bit as the Wembley Arena). There must've been a kid from the Repton on the bill that night as our seats were more or less ringside, and there was an East End fight promoter sitting in front of us who my dad hated for some reason. He was bald on top with ginger hair at the sides and I'm sure his name will come to me in a moment . . . Mickey Duff, that was him, though I don't think that was his real name as he was from Polish stock originally.

Anyway, Duff was talking to a black boxer called Billy Knight and another promoter we didn't know, and he was 'giving it the big I am' in the way some promoters will. Then my dad overheard him saying, 'My meat will fight your body any time' – meaning that some bout or other was on. Now my dad loved boxers, really respected them, and he wasn't going to have them talked about in such a disrespectful way. So he piped up from the row behind: 'What did you say? What did you just fucking say? Is that how you talk about the fighters who get you a living?'

At that point my dad completely lost the plot and really gave it to this guy with both barrels while Billy Knight stood there listening, open-mouthed. By the end of the exchange it was clear that someone was going to have to move. We stayed, they went . . . but don't worry, the iron bar isn't coming into this for a while yet. I'm just establishing the atmosphere of the evening.

All the way home in the car, my dad was still bubbling with anger: 'That's the kind of slags fight promoters are,' he kept saying, 'that's how they use people.' I don't know if he'd had bad experiences with them himself when he was younger, because it's not the kind of thing we would have talked about, but I don't suppose you can rule out that possibility.

When we got back from Wembley to Church Street – and this was bad timing on everyone's part – there were a group of bikers blocking the entrance to the same alley where the first incident with the iron bar had taken place. I don't know what they were doing there as none of our neighbours were bikers as far as we knew, but there were about fifteen of them, with ages ranging from twenty going up to about forty.

The Old Man pulls round into the alley to park, and at first he doesn't see them. But as we get out of the car to go into the house, one of the bikers blocks his way and says, 'You nearly fucking knocked me over.'

I'm shitting myself a bit now thinking, 'Don't just wade in, Dad, we're on a hiding to nothing here.' But never mind the odds not being exactly in our favour, after the night my dad's had, I already know it's gonna go off. 'No, son,' he says to this biker. 'I didn't nearly knock you over. If I'd have wanted to knock you over, I'd have fucking knocked you over, so get out of the fucking way.'

The guy does what he's told, but as we walk on towards the house, the biggest of the bikers gets off his bike and says, 'Who are you fucking talking to?' By this time I'm already moving towards the gate where the iron bar is, because I've seen how it's done and they're more than mob-handed. At this point, the biker's gone to throw a punch at my dad, and my Old Man's hit him with a left hook of such force that the biker's just gone down where he stood.

The geezer hits the ground so hard that you could see the dust come up in the glare of the streetlight. I know that sounds like something from a film, but I swear on my life it's what I saw. I think Scorsese's *Raging Bull* is the only movie that's ever got the impact of that kind of punch right, and De Niro didn't have an iron bar to hand either.

Before the biker's even finishing bouncing up off the ground, my dad's taken the iron bar off me. This other guy's already coming at him – a black fella as it happened, which was unusual for a biker – and my dad's knocked the teeth out of his head with the bar. Next thing I know he's got the fella on the floor beating him round the ribs saying, 'If you ever come back, I'll fucking kill you.' Needless to say, the lot of 'em fucked off – I've never seen a crowd disperse so quickly – and we never saw their leather jackets in that alley ever again.

That iron bar could do a lot of damage to people, and my dad knew how to go to work with it. I'm not saying this because I want to glorify these actions, but because that was the atmosphere I was brought up in. For a particular generation which came out of post-war England, that's what was handed down to us. You had to get on with people working on the markets, but if someone came down and wanted it then you had to be able to dish some out, otherwise people would walk all over you. My dad wasn't a gangster, but you don't fuck with family people either.

I suppose by telling these stories I am condoning them in a way. I do regret my dad being in a position where he felt he had to do those things to protect me, but I understand where the impulse to do them came from. I'm not being PC about this because fuck it, that was our way of life, and the idea that these people got what they fucking deserved is embedded quite deep within me. I know that's not necessarily the right way to think, and it's something I've tried to change over the years – not so that your family doesn't come first, but just because you don't want the aggravation.

Some of the success I've had as an actor has probably been down to the fact that when people see me in those kinds of situations in films, they believe I've been in them in real life, which I have been. The sequence in *Scum* where I have to hit Baldy with the iron bar was one of the easiest I've ever had to do, because I'd seen it happen, and not too long before either. A lot of people might've been shocked by what went on in that film, but I certainly wasn't.

I was nineteen going on twenty when we made the TV version of *Scum* in early 1977, and twenty-one going on twenty-two by the time we remade it for the cinema in 1979 after the first one was banned from being shown on the BBC. Although the second film is basically the same script as the first but with some extra violence and swearing added, the first is by far the scarier of the two in my opinion.

We're all just babies really at that stage, so you get more of a sense of the terrible things kids will do to other kids, and the ways grown men will manipulate them. By the time we got to do the film, which was cobbled together on more of a money basis, we were young men instead of boys, and it was a stretch to imagine that we were in borstal rather than an adult prison.

A lot of water, and other drinks, would pass under the bridge in my life between the two *Scums*. A fair proportion of those fluids would be taken in establishments run by a mate of mine called Neville Cole. His brother Eamon was Tony Yeates's godfather (in the being-there-at-your-christening sense, not in the mafia sense) and they were a couple of really good boxers who ran pubs and clubs. They used to have a big black fella who knocked about with them, a really nice bloke whose name was Tiny. Well, I don't suppose that was what it said on his birth certificate, but that was what we all called him.

Neville's original place was the Salmon and Ball. It was, and is, just down the road from the Repton, on the corner of Cambridge Heath and Bethnal Green Road – by the tube station where the terrible disaster happened in the Blitz. Neville changed the name to Tipples for a while. Locals would pronounce that in the proper East End style with a hard 'p' that was more like a 'b', so it sounded more like you were saying a cat's name than somewhere you'd want to go to have a pint.

Me and Tony Yeates saw a geezer put a gun to someone's head in there, once. We were only young fellas at the time – seventeen or eighteen at most – and we were in there having a Sunday lunchtime drink when we noticed two smart old boys and a couple of young 'uns sitting together. There was some uneasy laughter and then it all kind of went quiet. We looked round and saw that one of the young fellas had pulled out a gun and put it to the old boy's head. I say the old boy, but he was probably in his fifties – the same age as me now.

The young guy never swore at him, he just said, 'If you dig me out, I'll blow your head off.' The old guy replied, 'Come on, son, there's no need for that – we was just having a laugh.' A silence followed that seemed to last quite a long time, then the kid put his gun away and got up and left. There was no shouting and screaming or calling the police. Everyone just went back to their drinks.

After a while Neville opened up another place down on the Mile End Road, near Trinity Green. He set it up with a geezer called Martin Nash, and I only realised recently that this was probably where they got the name Nashville's from. My mind must have been on higher things at the time. There was certainly no one in there wearing rhinestones, although the odd cowboy might have put in an appearance.

For my money, quite a lot of which I spent in there, Nashville's was the best club in London. The vibe of it was somewhere between an East End disco and a piano lounge. Me and Tony Yeates were in there on the opening night and we were in there when it closed, and we had a lot of good times in between. The only note of sadness in these memories is that we lost Neville Cole a couple of years ago. He was a good man, and him dying would've been sad enough even if he hadn't won the fucking Lottery a while before he died. The truth of the old phrase 'You can't take it with you' was never more starkly or harshly demonstrated.

CHAPTER 17

BENJY'S NIGHTCLUB, MILE END

Neville and Martin really used to look after us. They were running things, and we were the kids on the firm. Being in that role in a group always tends to get you a fair bit of piss-taking, and we were no exception. One day they took me and Tony aside and told us they'd booked a champagne table for us down at Benjy's nightclub in Mile End as a 'little treat from the boys'. They said there were a couple of nice girls who wanted to meet us. Obviously, we knew how to pull a bird, but we weren't the type of kids to look a gift horse (or a gift bird) in the mouth, so we were there on time with bells on. Of course the two girls who turned up were both geezers – how were we to know Thursday was gay night?

That kind of thing is part of growing up, and Neville and Martin didn't mean it cruelly – either to us or the two gay guys. As it turns out, Tony and his mate have been very happy together. (Only joking, Tony, I know the cracks are starting to show.) Benjy's has had more name changes than West Ham have had away kits in the thirty-five years since, but last time I looked it was still hanging on, despite the council's best attempts to relieve it of its licence.

If Neville and Martin were ideal mentors when it came to East London nightlife, which they were, I was going to need someone to do the same job for me when it came to acting on film. And I couldn't have asked for anyone better than Alan Clarke. OK, I'd got the part in *Scum* because I had a boxer's walk, but I had no agent and no idea of what I was getting into.

The original TV version was a two-bob fucking BBC production where you had to get down to London Bridge under your own steam and then get the train down to Redhill. There was some messing about on that train which I can't even tell you about, but let's just say if the kids from *Scum* got in your carriage, you probably knew they were there. I think they based the kids from *Fame* on us, only we never wore the leg-warmers (though we could have done with them in a way, because it was freezing fucking cold on that set). Once we got there, we didn't really have too much idea of the kind of thing we were making, as Clarkey was keeping it all together in quite a secretive way to get what he wanted out of us.

I felt comfortable being around the Anna Scher boys, but they were their own gang and I wasn't part of it, which suited how I was and was also good for the film. We became mates over the years, but they were from North London. Now, Islington might not look a long way from the East End on the map, but the possibility that they might be Arsenal or Spurs supporters did not sit comfortably with me (Phil Daniels even supported Chelsea, for some reason which he was never able to adequately explain). It probably made it easier for me to be around a load of guys who never really acted like they were actors. I can't speak on their behalf, but I don't think most of us even booked that as our job description.

The performance I gave in *Scum* (and the later film version which more people have seen and is basically a cinematic Xerox of the first one) was purely down to Clarkey. He got the anger out of me, and I suppose the cunning, but what was really clever was the way he made it look like I was aware of what I was doing technically, even though I wasn't. I was on the screen a long time in those films for an actor with so little experience, and left to my own devices I would have had no idea of how to pace what I was doing. It was Alan who made sure I did what I did in the right places so the whole thing hung together properly.

Alan Clarke was an Evertonian, a tall, skinny guy with a scar on one side of his face, which I think he got from falling on a step outside a pub drunk, but that's his story, not mine. The best introduction to his character would be a tale he told me about him and Roy Minton (the writer of *Scum*). They were both quite fiery individuals, to put it mildly, and once they were coming down in a lift at the BBC when an argument came to blows. Basically, they're having a fight in this lift – eyes wide, nostrils flaring – then when it reaches the ground floor and the doors open, who should be outside but Moshe Dayan? The Israeli military leader and foreign minister – who was famous for the eye patch he had to wear after a sniper's bullet smashed some binoculars he was using – had obviously seen some brutal conflicts in his time, but Alan never told me if he tried to intervene in this one.

The most important thing I learned from Alan was that putting a performance together in a film is all about the moments where you demonstrate your power as a character. You're telling a story that might stretch over a year of someone's life or even longer, and you've got to compress a man's whole emotional appearance changing into an hour and a half. I wasn't capable of structuring that believably on my own because no one had ever taught me how to do it. Of course, I didn't see how much Alan was shaping what I was doing at the time. It took me a long while to actually develop some discipline about acting, and only once I'd done that did I realise the extent of Alan's influence. That's the mark of a clever teacher, when you are learning things without realising it.

I never forgot the way he went to work with me. There were moments when he'd just whisper in my ear and make me very calm and relaxed by saying, 'Don't worry about them, just concentrate on what you're doing.' Then there were other times when he'd say, 'You're fucking me about here', and that would upset me, because I had a lot of respect for him. Obviously, he was just saying that to wind me up, but it worked because I'd get really fucking mad.

I've learnt to use that technique on myself over the years. Sometimes on a set even now I'll call myself a cunt or whatever to liven myself up. It's the acting equivalent of having Jackie Bowers in your corner. The director might think I'm angry with him when he hears me grumbling away to myself, so I'll have to explain that I'm not being horrible, I just talk to myself a lot before a scene. It's funny sometimes when I come out of it to see other actors looking at me as if to say, 'Well, what's the matter with you?'

Most of what you're taught at drama college relates to the theatre rather than cinema, so you have to kind of start from scratch once you make that shift. Being in front of a camera never worried me in itself. Of course, the first thing people will tell you is: 'Forget about the camera. Don't even think about it, just do what you do.' I actually found that advice very easy to follow at first. 'I'm not going to worry about the camera, let the camera worry about me' was the way I approached it.

Ignorance is bliss on a film set, because when you've got no idea of what's happening, you can just get on with it. Things only start to get complicated once you learn more about the technical side – what the different lenses are and how close the shots are going to be. That's when you start to second-guess yourself. One minute you feel perfectly at home, and then you know too much. Suddenly your only option is to relearn how not to be aware of the camera by making the knowledge you've picked up work for you on a technical level without it looking like that's a conscious process. That's when acting becomes a whole different game.

One thing I would say is that the old saying that the camera never lies is bullshit, because it does. I've done things I thought were blinding and when I've seen them played back they were shit. It works the other way too, but when you watch something you thought was going to be terrible and it actually works, that's normally because the director, for whatever reason, didn't let you in on what they were trying to get.

The most important thing when you're shooting out of sequence – which is how it's normally done – is learning to sort the script out in your head as you're going along. People often think it must be difficult to do things in a different order to how they're seen, but it can actually work out better that way. For example, if you do the end before anything else, you understand where you've got to get to and you can start to think about all the different shapes you can put in along the road. In other films – *Nil by Mouth* would be a good example – you don't need to have so much of a journey through it so you can just play each moment and not worry about the next one.

Alan Clarke was well known for having a clear political agenda, and as my little disagreement with Vanessa Redgrave showed, I wasn't always in tune with left-wing opinions. If anything, my family background pushed me more to the right. Even though he's working-class, my dad would always vote Tory.

Some people find that difficult to understand, but there's a long tradition of grafters who run their own businesses being quite right-wing – Margaret Thatcher's dad was a grocer after all. You've worked hard to get what you've got and you don't like the idea of other people getting something for nothing. I can appreciate and even agree with that opinion, but my political views have never been quite as fixed as my dad's were.

Sometimes I'll watch documentaries about working-class people fighting for their rights and see the kind of conditions they lived in and think, 'Dad, what were you talking about?' I'm not saying I've got more left-wing as I've got older, but maybe I've moved a bit closer to the middle of the road. Socialism doesn't add up in my mind, but it wouldn't make sense for me to be a Tory either. After all, both sides of my family came out of the workhouse, and the Conservatives are the kind of fuckers who put us in there. You can't say that's not a conflict of interest, so why should I fucking vote for them now?

As a rule I try to judge individual issues and political personalities on their merits. What I look for is that quite rare brand of politician who makes an honest attempt to do what he or she has said they're gonna do. They don't necessarily have to succeed, they just have to give it a go. The other mob – the ones who promise one thing and then do something totally different the minute they get in power – are much more numerous. But as far as I'm concerned they should be held to account under the Trades Descriptions Act, the same way a butcher who sold you venison which was actually horse would be.

All of this is a roundabout way of saying that I didn't really have a problem with the underlying politics of *Scum*, which were what a lot of the controversy surrounding the film was about. I didn't view it so much as a political thing of left versus right. For me it was a simple matter of people who were in authority – whether that was the warders or the other boys – treating the kids who were under them like shit.

We bang kids up in these fucking conditions, but at the end of the day whatever you've done you're supposed to go into the system to be rehabilitated, and that just wasn't the way it worked at the time. What you see happening in *Scum* is more about punishment, and while I do think there are certain people who need to be punished, it's not a good principle to run the whole system on.

Because of the *Scum* connection I was invited to Rodney Wing at HM Prison Portland a few years after the film came out to see the work they were doing there trying to rehabilitate people. The idea was to come in and have a chat with the kids and try to do a theatre group with them – just to give them the idea that if I can do it, maybe you can too. I must admit I was very apprehensive about doing this at first. I just thought, 'Fuck me, some of these kids are probably in here for murder. How am I going to help them become better people just by doing a bit of acting?'

In a way, I still think that. But when I saw what those warders were trying to do by sitting the kids around and talking about their problems, I started to see the potential of it. They were trying to do something really proper but – and sadly this is how it always works with human beings – the screws in the grown-up nick next door didn't want anything to do with it. Their mentality was: 'We're here to punish these people, and that's what we're gonna do.' Never mind how many statistics might show them that these kids are much less likely to be a danger to others when they go back out on the street if someone's actually given them a chance.

Wherever you stand on this, there's no denying that the reason the criminal justice system should exist in the first place – which is to rehabilitate people so they won't commit any more crimes – has kind of got lost as more and more of the system's energies go towards defending its own status quo. You could see that very clearly in the way the political establishment clamped down on *Scum*. It was like the film itself was the rebel character Archer – played by David Threlfall in the first version and Mick Ford in the second – and Parliament and the BBC were the screws.

Of course, I wasn't overly bothered about all this at the time. I had enough going on in my life not to be too invested in it. So, in the autumn of 1977, when the original TV *Scum* actually got banned – which for all I knew meant my first leading role was going to go forever unseen – I just thought, 'Well, there you go', and effectively retired from the acting business for eighteen months.

I'll get onto how I made ends meet in the next few chapters, but obviously there was a fair amount of rebellion in the air in that particular Jubilee year. I didn't dress like a punk – the safety-pin gear wasn't for me, although the drainpipe trousers were alright – but I liked the Sex Pistols' music. Live gigs still didn't really interest me though. I went up the Marquee Club once and got in a big row with some pogo-ers, and that was about the end of it. If you'd told me that within two or three years, not only would Sid Vicious be dead but I'd have acted with all three of his surviving bandmates, I would probably have been a bit surprised.

One musical opportunity I wasn't going to pass up in the meantime was the chance to DJ for nurses' parties. They love a dance, don't they, nurses? And everyone knows that it's any patriotic Englishmen's duty to try to bring happiness to as many nurses as possible.

How this important landmark in DJing history came about was that Tony Yeates was working as a photographer at St Thomas' Hospital by this time – taking photos of all the operations for their records. He was, and is, a really good smudger (as photographers were always called on my plot), and it was an interesting job, if a bit gory. He took some amazing pictures of surgeons' hands as well, and when someone offered him the chance to fake a different kind of dexterity by DJing for a nurses' party, Tony was hardly going to say no.

'Don't worry, I'll do it,' he'd told them. 'Me and my mate Ray have got all the equipment.' Of course we ain't got any of the equipment, and we ain't got any DJing experience either, but if Tony Blackburn can do this, how hard can it be?

Luckily, Tony's younger brother Steve had some turntables we could borrow for the night, and we also borrowed Steve, who came along to show us how to use them. We set off for deepest darkest South London in an optimistic frame of mind, blissfully ignorant of the fact that there's a mob out of Brixton who had the job before us and got sacked, who are not best pleased about losing their gig to a couple of East London pumpkins. So we're in there on the night, making it up as we go along with all the nurses having a great time dancing to our random selection of old singles. (I remember Rod Stewart's 'Maggie May' going down particularly well. 'Mr Blue Sky' by ELO was another winner – that was about as up to the minute as we got.) Then we look over to see this angry-looking black guy with a big velvet pimp hat on standing at the back with all his cronies.

The message somehow gets through to us that this used to be their gig. Tony goes, 'It's on us,' and I'm thinking, 'Uh-oh. We've nicked their gig, on their manor – we're in trouble here.' It seems like whatever's gonna happen is probably gonna happen, so I go for the 'in for a penny, in for a pound' strategy, and put on that song 'Kung Fu Fighting' – Carl Douglas, I think it was – with a special dedication: 'And this is for the pimp and his mates at the back.'

They're all getting a bit lively at this point but nothing actually happens, so I'm thinking, 'We might have fronted 'em here.' It's only me, Tony and his kid brother with all this expensive DJ equipment which we've got to get back in the motor, because if things had gone off that would've probably been the first casualty of war. So, at the end of the night we pile it all into this green Triumph Herald estate we'd picked up from somewhere which you could only start with a screwdriver.

As we pull away, we look round and see three car-loads of this mob following us. A car chase ensues, only it's more like *Steptoe and Son* than *Smokey and the Bandit* (which was on at the pictures that year) because we're staggering along in this knackered old Triumph throwing records out of the window at them for a laugh – only the pony ones, not The Jam or anything like that. They finally catch up with us around the back of the Italia Conti stage school in Farringdon.

At this point we'd be very happy to discover that the whole thing is some kind of on-location improvisation workshop, but sadly that doesn't look likely. I ask Tony if he's ready, he nods, and we get out of the car. These geezers are all around us and they're more than mob-handed, so I go up to the guy in the pimp hat and say, 'Alright, mate. There's obviously enough of you to do us, but are we men? Put up your two best, me and him [I'm pointing at Tony now because Stephen was only a little fella and we wanted to keep him out of it] will fight them, and whoever wins, wins.'

Now I'm clutching at straws here, but we ain't got no chance otherwise, and the tactic seems to be working because they're back-tracking a bit – it's like they're not sure about us. Taking advantage of their moment of hesitation, I go round to the back of the car, because I know I've got an iron bar in my bag and they're not gonna want to fight one-on-one with that. The minute I reach in the car to pull it out, they think I've got a shooter. One of them shouts, 'He's got a gun', and it's just starting to feel like we might get out of this alive when another car pulls up and another big black guy gets out.

This geezer's a mountain and we're thinking, 'Oh fuck! We're for it now.' He comes up to us asking, 'What's the trouble, boys?' So, trying to keep calm because I don't know who this guy is or what his connection is to the other mob, I go, 'Nothing, mate – the boys are just putting it on us a bit.' At that point he turns round to them and goes, 'You fucking lot, get outta here.' He's literally the biggest black man in the world and he's telling them to fuck off, which they promptly do.

It turned out not to be a black and white thing to him on any level. They were a gang who were picking on us, and he was just a nice guy passing through who saw three kids in trouble and decided to help us out. We shook his hand with a big sigh of relief, in fact I gave him a grateful cuddle, then off we all went into the Clerkenwell night. Result! In fact, a Triumph, although strangely enough Stephen never offered to lend us his DJ equipment again ...

CHAPTER 18

THE 277 BUS UP
BURDETT ROAD

I had some funny old motors in my first few years of driving round London. I knew nothing about cars whatsoever, but I did have a happy knack for getting hold of dodgy MOTs, which wasn't just useful but vital given the state of some of the heaps I was at the wheel of.

I'd done most of my learning to drive in a knackered Ford Anglia van with a big long gear-stick. I used to have a problem going round corners in it because there was something about the layout of the pedals which encouraged you to put your foot on the accelerator rather than the brake. That's never a good idea, especially when it nearly turns the whole thing on its side, and even more so when that happens on the rare occasion when you've persuaded your dad to take you for a driving lesson (admittedly I had already driven the car around on my own or with mates a fair bit before it was strictly legal). This mistake got me thrown out of the driver's seat with a clump round the side of the head as a bonus and my dad drove home saying, 'I ain't getting in a bloody car with you again.'

On the set of *That Summer!* in 1978.

Shadow-boxing with my mate Tony London on the beach at Torquay – Elaine made the right choice.

They called Esther Williams 'A Goddess when wet'...

In *Quadrophenia* with my leathers and my Liberace haircut.

On honeymoon in the Canary Islands with Elaine and a camel.

We got straight off the plane home and went to the premiere of *Scum* – note the suitcases and my *Quadrophenia* badge.

The concluding riot in *Scum* – no need for Phil Daniels to help me out here.
I was the Daddy by this time . . .

Luckily make-up doesn't sting like a real shiner.

My dad at the bar in Church Street, Enfield – no sign of the Bobby Moore World Cup ice bucket for some reason.

'Black Magic, Raymond?' – 'Don't mind if I do'.

This is the outfit I wore on that plane trip to Cannes with Alan Clarke – not sure if the 'foot up' thing is quite working for me, though.

At the Edinburgh Film Festival with *Scum* in 1979.

In Canada in 1980 filming *Ladies And Gentlemen, the Fabulous Stains.* Clockwise from top left: a) With Paul Simonon b) A beery leer c) With Steve Jones d) Elaine offers me a lesson in microphone technique e) Onstage as lead singer of 'The Looters' f) Elaine is the meat in a Laura Dern/Marin Kanter sandwich g) Paul Cook shows how a Sex Pistol occupies a chair.

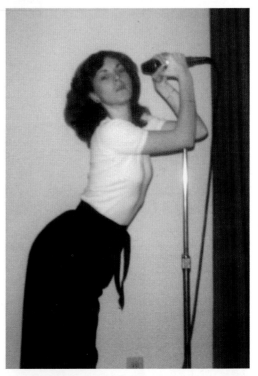

Me with Alex Steene, John Conteh and Perry Fenwick, who plays Billy Mitchell in *EastEnders*. He's a great mate of mine who comes from my manor. Well, close enough . . . Canning Town/Custom House.

Even Will Scarlet needs a fag break.

The face that launched a thousand arrows . . .

Lois with me, mum and Toffy, and then getting christened with me and Elaine.

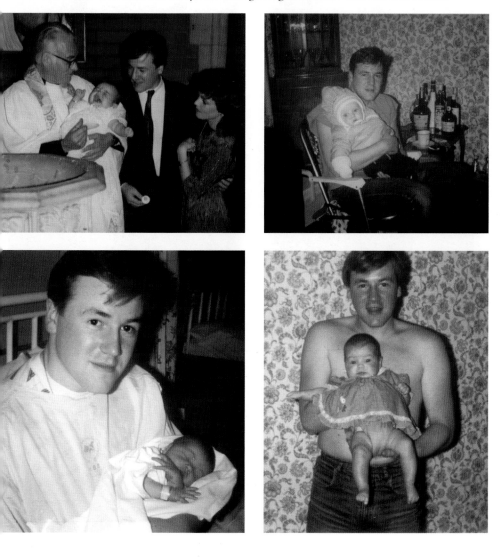

Matthew McConaughey struggles not to look intimidated by my manly physique.

The leafy suburbs of Winchmore Hill was where I took my driving tests. One of the times I failed, the examiner did me on driving too close to parked vehicles. I asked him, 'Did I hit any?' He answered, 'No', so I said, 'Well, how can I have been too fucking close then?' And yet still I failed – where was the justice? There might have been a bit of an altercation after that – I was going through a bit of a hot-headed phase – and I eventually passed at the third time of asking. I don't know how because that was probably the worst I'd ever driven in my life. Maybe the examiners just wanted to get rid of me.

Their plan worked, because as soon as I could get out of Enfield under my own steam, that place didn't see me for dust. I'd had a few trial runs down to Whitechapel and Stratford on my dad's moped. He was in the process of giving up on the fruit and veg game by that point because the big supermarket chains had killed it, and was doing the Knowledge to become a black-cab driver.

He already knew London like the back of his hand, so he passed the test really quickly, but while he was going round studying his little clipboard with a map on it in the daylight hours, I used to sneak into the garden of an evening and borrow his bike to head off to the East End. It was best not to get caught, because he still wasn't the biggest fan of two-wheeled transportation, but he couldn't really say too much about it now he was off out on a bike all day himself.

Once I started to get my hands on vehicles of my own, I loved the sense of freedom I felt bombing back home through Hackney and then up the A10. I had an old claret Cortina for a while (all it needed was some blue trim and the colour scheme would've been perfect). There was a side-window missing which I'd had to replace with some plastic, and one wing was all bent back where I'd hit something. Overall that car was a total rust-bucket, but it did used to go. Then there was the Triumph Herald estate which got us out of the sticky DJing situation, and last but not least was a black Triumph Herald convertible which I borrowed for a long time. That one only started with a screwdriver as well, but it was so worn you had to physically turn the whole ignition. I think in the end only the wires were left.

The places I'd be going to would be Moro's or the Two Puddings in Stratford, or a pub called the Charleston further over towards Maryland Point. Obviously it was the height of the disco era, but although I'd loved Motown and early seventies soul, I wasn't so into disco. I still learnt how to use the music to my advantage. If John Travolta and The Bee Gees could, then why shouldn't I? But I wasn't having the fashion. When the big round collars and the stack-heeled shoes came in I wore them once. That night I slipped on some ice on the platform of Bruce Grove station and to my embarrassment fell down onto the track – fucking stack-heels! No, thank you very much – it was back to the old straight jeans and winkle-pickers for me.

Our status as nightlife apprentices on Martin Nash and Neville Cole's firm broadened our range of places to go out as well. I re-member hearing an enormous crash outside Tipples once. We ran into the street to see a car more or less cut in half and Neville getting out of it with one of the Hariths, who were a big family from another area. They were both all bruised and cut up, but they just walked into the pub and said, 'Come on, we're going to Beirut.'

That's what we called the Old Kent Road in South London, because when you went down there at the weekend, all you'd hear was sirens. On the night in question we got in another motor and drove to Le Connoisseur, which was a Greek restaurant but with a club above it. I remember going to use the toilet in this bar and looking up to see a camera pointing at me. I suppose it was there to stop people snorting Charlie, but that wasn't the purpose of my visit. I went back out there and told everyone, 'There's a camera in the khazi', and they all went, 'No!'

The number of stabbings on the Old Kent Road was outrageous in those days. Someone would say, 'We're going over Beirut on Saturday', and you'd just think, 'Oh for fuck's sake!' You'd want to come back to Bethnal Green for a bit of peace and quiet . . . yeah, right.

It was buzzing on the weekends in E2 at that time too. There were a lot of good pubs, and if you'd pulled and you wanted to take a bird out on your own, the place me and Tony Yeates would always go to was the Venus steakhouse in Bethnal Green Road. I'd always have the same meal in there: start with a prawn cocktail (it was the seventies after all), then T-bone steak, obviously, and a bottle of that Portuguese fizzy rosé to help it go down.

I know what you're thinking – 'That's a well-oiled seduction machine' – and, to be honest, it was. But things didn't always go to plan in that department, especially when you went off your usual manor. And even more so if you couldn't get hold of a car, so public transport had to be factored in.

The incident I'm about to describe definitely took place between the two *Scums*, because I was going to a party with Ray Burdis and some of the other Anna Scher guys I'd got to know on the first one, and by the time the second one came out I'd met my Elaine and was safely off the market. At this particular point in time I'd just split up with a bird, so I wasn't going out with anyone, but I'd met this beautiful-looking girl through a family connection with my auntie Jeanie.

I'm not going to say what her name was, because she's a married woman now and it'll be embarrassing for her, but she lived in the flats round the back of the Londoner pub in Limehouse. I went round there to pick her up and knocked on her parents' door: 'Hello, Mr and Mrs —, I'm Raymond' – all very polite and wanting to make a good impression.

They were the same way: 'Hello, Raymond, come in.' Unfortunately, there was a telephone on the floor of the hallway which I didn't see, and as I walked towards the front room I accidentally kicked it – still on its cord – straight through the plate-glass door to the lounge.

At this point, obviously, I'm mortified. The door is smashed to smithereens, there's little bits of glass everywhere, and I'm saying, 'I'm so sorry, I didn't see the phone', and trying to help them clear up the mess. The girl I'm waiting to go out with is still upstairs getting ready, but her mum and dad are being really nice about it: 'Don't worry, Raymond. Sit yourself down and we'll make you up a nice cup of tea.' They show me to a seat and go off to the kitchen to put the kettle on, but as I lean back on the sofa, the arm splits and falls off. I'm desperately trying to get it back on while they're still out of the room but it just won't hold, so when they come back I just have to say, 'I'm sorry, I've broken your settee.'

Of course, by this time they're looking at me like I'm some sort of nutter. Fucking hell, it's embarrassing. Luckily, at that point their daughter's finally got herself ready, and we set off to get a bus up to the tube at Mile End (normally I'd have got a cab, so I must have been skint). We get on the old 277 and go upstairs, and now the pain of what's happened is starting to fade a bit – I'm not completely over it, but we're having a nice chat.

At this point a Russian sailor comes up the stairs – in full uniform, that's how I can see he's a Ruskie. He walks over and starts talking to us in broken English, but it's clear enough that his intentions aren't honourable.

'You and your girlfriend come with me and we'll have a good night,' he says. I go, 'We'll have a what?' There's no other way this is going to go after that than with the two of us having a fight, and I end up giving the Russian a good fucking hiding right there, on the top deck.

The bus driver's going potty, so we have to get off the bus and walk the rest of the way up to Mile End. Now that's three really bad things that have happened in the space of twenty minutes. We should have quit while we were behind, but we didn't, and for a little while things started to run a bit more smoothly again. We got the tube over to where the party was – in one of those big three-storey houses in Cloudesley Square, on the posh side of Islington.

I've bought a bottle of something. They've let us in fine and we've gone straight upstairs to the front room. I'm having a quick word with my mates. My date doesn't know anyone, but she's having a nice chat with the girls, and I'm keeping half an eye on her the whole time to make sure she's doing alright. Then I look up to see her walking towards me and everything goes into slow motion – always a bad sign with me.

The reason everything goes into slow motion on this occasion is because she's tripped on the carpet, and I can see she's falling towards the marble fireplace. I stick my arm out to grab her, and in that fraction of a second, just as I'm sighing with relief because I've saved the day, my elbow knocks into this huge cut-glass chandelier which for some reason is sitting on the table. First, it rocks – but I can't catch it because I've still got Lucky in my arms – then it falls. And then it hits the marble fireplace and shatters into even more pieces than the door into her lounge did about an hour before.

The host of the party is screaming at me, understandably enough, and I'm trying to explain that I'm very, very sorry, but my friend was falling and I couldn't let her hit her head. We've only been there ten minutes and we've hardly had a drink, but I'm telling her I'll pay for the damage – even though I don't know how, 'cos I've not got more than a tenner on me. By this time the lady of the house is right up in my face shouting, 'Son, if you work from now till Doomsday, you won't be able to afford that fucking light', and I'm saying, 'I think we'd better leave', because now I'm starting to get angry.

Me and the Typhoid Mary of Limehouse had quite a good chat on the tube home, but we never went out together again. She was a lovely girl and everything, but I think on balance we realised that it probably wasn't meant to be.

Not all of my misadventures when it came to girls were quite so much like something out of a romantic comedy. Once we had wheels Tony Yeates and I would go all over East London and Essex in pursuit of a bird, and there was one time in Southend when we both caught crabs at the seaside. We'd nicked the bouncers' girlfriends at a club called the Zero 6, which got its name from the runway at Southend airport that it was sitting right at the end of. They used to play Donald Byrd and the Blackbyrds' 'Flight Time' as their theme song at that place, because it had some great plane noise sound-effects in it. They should've handed out some peanuts and a face towel as you came in to complete the effect, really.

Naturally, the bouncers weren't too happy about what we were up to, and they had a little go at us outside, but we had it away a bit lively and everything was sweet. The two girls took us back to their place and we did what we done – boom boom boom boom. The next day they cooked us Sunday dinner. The two bob went in the gas, then it went off again after we'd eaten and we had a swoppo – which is the opposite of a stoppo.

A week after returning home, we'd both got crabs. There was no way of knowing which of the girls had given them to us – it could've been both of them. Either way, we had no idea what to fucking do about it.

I shaved all the hair off my bollocks, but that didn't do any good and the stubble growing back is the worse thing in the world – worse even than the crabs themselves. Then Tony did some research and got us some blue ointment – 'unction' I think it was called – and they all jumped off, pyong . . . job done.

One night not long after that we were standing in a club at the Seven Kings. It was one of those places where the UV lights give everyone a blue tinge, and this geezer we were talking to had a crab crawling across his eyebrows. They've got a kind of black dot in them – almost like a pin head – and once you've had a visitation you're not going to have any trouble recognising one, especially when it's floodlit by ultra-violet. We both looked at this geezer with his un-wanted guest on his face and we both looked at each other and we were out of there before he'd finished his sentence.

Although I was out and about a lot at this time, I'd still usually be back in Enfield for Sunday dinner (unless I had a better offer on the Essex Riviera, of course). Even now I like to get the family together for a big meal at least once a week if everyone's about. If we've got guests I have to warn them that we don't stand on ceremony. Don't blink at the wrong moment or everyone else will have had all the best roast potatoes.

Of course, bringing people together to eat can cause friction as well as harmony, especially when you're dealing with a family who all have quick tempers. We did have our moments around that Church Street dinner table. Mum and Dad would be sat at either end with me and Laura bickering across the table. Once she got the hump so badly over something I'd said that she threw her knife at me across the table. It stuck right in my sternum and kind of wobbled a bit like a knife-thrower's in a cartoon would. I remember looking down in disbelief to see it fall to the table and a little trickle of blood flowing down my white shirt.

I went garrity and dived at her across the table, then she dived back at me and we're strangling each other, and by the time my mum and dad have got their arms round our necks trying to stop us, we look like one of those Tasmanian Devil cartoons where a fight almost becomes a cloud. Even the dog's going mental. Brandy's gone to the big kennel in the sky by that point, so it's a little Jack Russell called Ben who's barking his head off. In the ensuing melee one of my legs goes through the French windows and gets quite badly cut, but there's no sulking in my house. Something happens and then it's over – done. Twenty minutes later, we're all sitting on the sofa holding hands and watching the Sunday film together.

I clearly remember that film as being *The Champ* because I've got a mental picture of us all holding hands and crying at the scene near the end where Jon Voight's boxer dies (an event which was always going to tug at the heart-strings of the Winstone household). The little kid's going, 'Champ, wake up! Wake up!' My mum's crying, my dad's crying, I'm crying, Laura's crying – even the dog's crying. But that film didn't come out until 1979 and I'd left home by the time it could've been on TV, so maybe I'd just come back for Sunday lunch a bit later on to reconnect with my family. It's good to stay in touch with your family, but not necessarily via a knife stuck in your chest.

I should say at this point that my sister Laura tells this story differently to the way I do. She insists she stabbed me with a fork, not a knife, but I think she's getting mixed up with another earlier occasion, when I'd showed her up in front of her mate and she went for me on the staircase. The only thing that comes back to me from that one is the excruciating pain of the fork she'd stuck in the back of my hand. All in all, there's a lot to be said for plastic cutlery.

There's also a lot to be said for kids who are ready to spread their wings getting the chance to do that, and I finally got my marching orders from the family home after an incident with a party which got a bit out of control. My mum and dad had gone on holiday, leaving strict instructions for me not to have a party. So, of course, I had to have one. It was the classic scenario of loads more people turning up than I'd expected, and by the end it did get a bit outrageous. There was talcum powder and baby oil everywhere – they trashed the gaff.

When I woke up in the morning and surveyed the devastation all around me through the fog of my brutal hangover, it was just like that old Yellow Pages advert where the kid goes, 'French polisher? It's just possible you could save my life . . .' Except there was no French polisher around to do the honours.

I did everything I could to tidy the place up, but it just wasn't within my power to put everything right. When my mum and dad came back and saw what had happened, that was me gone. I was angry with them for throwing me out at the time, but looking back it all worked out OK.

After a few nights of sleeping on different people's settees, I thought, 'Bollocks to this, I'm going to see Granddad', and went and moved in with Toffy, who was on his own by then and didn't mind the company. My mum and dad wanted him to kick me out so I'd have no choice but to come home, but he wouldn't do it. I think he could see that living with him was good for me – it gave me a bit more independence without leaving me completely on my own.

I might've been twenty by this time but I was still a bit wayward, and having a much older role model I loved and respected around wasn't going to do me any harm. Another upside was I got to live in Hackney for the next year or so – just over the road from the house I'd spent the first twelve months of my life in.

There's a postscript to the story which shows how much things have changed these days in terms of everyone knowing what everyone else is up to. On the night of my party a couple of mates who I'd gone to school with took two girls home with them and had a really bad car crash on the way out to Ware. Everyone survived but they all had to be cut out of the vehicle, and the two guys were in hospital in traction for months on end. But because my mum and dad kicked me out the next day and I went off to live with my granddad, I didn't find out what had happened till a year or so later.

I suppose as much as anything this tells you how happy I was to be back in the East End – it turned out that if you took the man out of Enfield you actually could take the Enfield out of the man (well, this one, anyway). But still, no one thought to ring and tell me. Obviously mobiles weren't in use yet – not even the giant ones we had in the eighties – so the next time I saw my mates a year or so later they were really angry with me. 'You fucker,' they said, 'we had a terrible car crash and you didn't even come and visit us.'

CHAPTER 19

GATSBY HOUSE

It's true what they say about your grandparents – sometimes you can talk to them in a way that you can't talk to your mum and dad. I've spoken to a lot of my mates who've said they were always drawn to their granddads, partly because they aren't there all the time, whereas your dad is so close to you that there will often be some kind of trouble either bubbling under or boiling over. It's unfair on dads in a way, but as you get older that competitive element about who is the guv'nor is always going to creep in.

There was none of that with my granddad Toffy. He still lived in the same two-bedroom council flat where he'd been on his own since Nanny Maud died a few years before. It was in an old-fashioned brick block called Gatsby House on the Frampton Park Estate, just east of Mare Street in Hackney. The name Gatsby tends to be associated with good living, and even though his circumstances were obviously less luxurious than Robert Redford's or Leonardo DiCaprio's in the films, Toffy always maintained his own elegant personal style.

This wasn't just about looking immaculate or lifting his hat to the ladies as he walked down the road – it went deeper. He was an absolute gent and living with him for a year was a great education in little things you shouldn't even have to think or talk about. As a result I will still open the door for a woman or stand up on a train to let her sit down, even now. Of course, nine times out of ten women are so independent that they'll just say, 'I'm alright, thank you', but that's no reason for me to stop making the effort.

Because I'd been so stubborn about not going back to my parents', I hadn't just lost my home, I'd got the sack from my job as well. Although I couldn't work with my dad on the markets any more, I didn't want to sign on and all that shit, so I ended up getting a job with Fred, a friend of his who ran a grocer's called Oliver Marcus in Muswell Hill. He was a good man, big Freddie. Even though he was my dad's mate, he wouldn't be pressured into giving me the old heave-ho so I'd have to go home like my dad wanted. Looking back, I put both Freddie and my granddad in a bit of a situation as far as my dad was concerned, but I was grateful that they both stuck up for me, and I suppose this made me feel like more of my own man in a way, which was probably what refusing to come back home was all about in the first place.

Every working day for about a year I travelled from Hackney to Muswell Hill to do my shift in that shop. I was happy to work there because I knew the fruit and veg game inside out by then. I didn't know the area, though. It was very . . . bohemian would be a good word. TV faces would come in all the time – Wilfred Pickles, he was a regular – and there were loads of poets and people like that as well. I know what you're thinking: 'Just Ray's home turf.'

I've always had an affinity with people from earlier generations, and I suppose going off to work in the shop all day, then coming home and maybe going to the pub with my granddad and his mates, I was living the life of someone much older than I actually was. Even when Tony Yeates and I were out and about in the clubs at that time, the older guys would be looking out for us. They certainly knew how to enjoy themselves, and that was true of my granddad as well. Neither of the two main pubs he used to go to is there any more, but one was called The North and the other was The Frampton Park Arms. I remember coming home late one night after I'd been to a party – creeping into the flat as quietly as I could so as not to wake him up at about three o'clock in the morning. Two hours later I heard the front door shutting quietly as Granddad came back from a lock-in.

As far as Granddad's work as a tic-tac man went, I never really got involved with it. That was his business and he just got on with it. He was still going all over the country when I lived with him – not just to Kempton and Sandown, but as far as York, Dublin, even Paris. Tic-tacking is another game which is pretty much over now. Mobile phones killed it. That's a shame because it was a big part of the excitement of going to the races, but I suppose the whole online betting thing has kind of expanded to fill the space.

The idea of having a flutter on your computer at home would've seemed like science fiction to us when we saw Lester time Roberto's run perfectly to win the Derby in 1972. And nothing had changed when I went to Epsom for the big race again in 1978. Lester had won on The Minstrel the year before, but he didn't win this time. Greville Starkey did. Six years on from the day-trip that ended my school career, I wasn't selling umbrellas any more, but my granddad was still tic-tacking, and Billy Brown and his firm who I knew from Chrisp Street Market were still down there too.

Granddad got mugged one day coming home from the races. He was a shrewd old boy in that he'd keep a couple of quid in his pocket and the rest he'd have tucked away. So when two guys followed him on the way back to the flats, he turned round and said, 'What do you want, son? Do you want a few quid off me? Well, that's all I've got. Rather than you give me a bashing, why not just take that?' And they did, so he came home unscathed with his wad of notes in his sock. All we could find out about the main mugger was that he had blond hair, so anyone we bumped into with blond hair was potentially in strife for a while from that point on.

My granddad had been no pushover as a younger man. Obviously he'd done his bit of boxing, and there was a story – which I know is true because the guy who ran the newsagent's confirmed it – about him going to the shop opposite the Frampton Park estate with one of my cousin's kids when they were still a baby. Someone barged to the front past a woman in the queue so Granddad called them on it: 'Mind out, son, you're pushing the lady there.' But the guy didn't apologise, so Granddad handed the baby to the woman and knocked him to the ground, then took the baby back, finished queuing for his paper and justice was done.

On a scale of general belligerence from one to ten, he'd have come a lot lower down than my dad, though. My dad, I'd say, was an eight (although some people might call him an eleven), but my granddad was no more than a three or four. His was the example that made me aspire to be a gentleman, not so much in the way you talk, but in the way you are with people and how you deal with them. I've changed my outlook on a lot of things over the years, but even now I'm still drawn to that idea of an unspoken moral code. It's not necessarily the strictness of it that I like, so much as the sense of everyone having respect for each other.

The atmosphere in that flat wasn't all uptight and old-fashioned. He was a very kind man, my granddad. The whole time we lived together, he did all the cooking. Once I'd made the mistake of telling him a particular meal was my favourite, I used to get it three times a week. The meal in question was a pork chop with some apple sauce, a grilled tomato, chips, baked beans and peas. I did like it at the time, but I ate a lifetime's supply of it in that year.

As well as having a generous spirit, Toffy was also an absolute character. He used to love talking to his goldfish. He'd say, 'That goldfish understands every word I say', and you'd be fairly sure he was joking, but not quite certain. He was also one of those people it's really good fun to play a prank on, and I used to wind him up something terrible.

One time, I was sitting up in the flat with my two cousins Melanie and Tracy. Mel was sitting on the floor and she had these big boots on, so while Granddad was out of the front room for a minute I said, 'Take your boots off and bend your legs back, then we'll put the boots up against your knees so it looks like your legs are stretching straight out.'

Granddad came back in, sat down in his armchair and started talking about his goldfish and the big fights the chivvy men – the men who carried chivs (razors or knives) – used to have at the races. All of a sudden, I just went mad. I threw myself at Mel and ripped one of the boots away so it looked like I'd pulled her leg off. Granddad went fucking apeshit. He was screaming, 'What have you done?' He was so relieved when we showed him her leg was still there that he actually forgot to be angry.

Another memorable occasion was the time Granddad and I went to visit my cousin Charlie in prison. The bright bubbly boy I used to knock about with at the Lansdowne Club had taken a few wrong turnings in the intervening years and got himself banged up for armed robbery. He got himself done for what's called a 'ready-eyed job' in Hatton Garden, which was an insurance caper where a guy on the inside actually wants it doing. Charlie went in when there was supposed to be no one about, but someone had made a boo-boo, and as it turned out there was a meeting going on, so they had to tie everyone up and take a bit of tom away. (Tomfoolery/jewellery – keep up.)

Instead of simply burying the stuff till the heat was off like any sensible person would, Charlie-boy put it on top of the wardrobe in his bedroom and bought himself a Mercedes. There weren't too many of them on the street in Hackney where he lived – just down the road from my granddad's flat, on the way to Victoria Park – so it attracted a bit of attention. In the end the Old Bill came round, and he got captured and sent down for a few years. He got it wrong, old Charlie-boy, and he paid a heavy price in the long run.

The day we went down to visit him in Maidstone prison, there was no sign of how sadly this story was going to pan out. Me and Granddad made it down to the station, probably London Bridge, to get the train to Maidstone, and on the platform there was a bloke done up as a cowboy, with the hat and the six-guns and everything. He had two birds in hot-pants with him, one on each arm. They were good sorts as well, which attracted my interest. I said to Granddad, 'Look at that, I wonder where they're going.'

Eventually the train pulls into Maidstone, we get off and of course the geezer and the two birds do too. You have to walk up the hill a bit to get to the prison, which is like an old castle. The bloke and the two birds are walking in front of us the whole way. When we all get there they take you into a little room at the side, where the guy takes out his six-guns – which I presume were toys, because real six-shooters wouldn't go down too well in a prison – twirls them in the old Western style and hands them over.

Granddad and me are laughing as we follow them into the nick because we can see what the geezer's up to. Visiting time at Maidstone is set up almost like a stage, with all the cons sitting there as the audience. You can imagine the reaction when he walks in there to visit his mate or his brother or whatever with the two birds in hot-pants – the whole place stands up and starts clapping, even the screws.

The other funny thing about prison visiting for me is that I'll always see someone else I know in there. This time it was Sammy McCarthy, the old boxer who used to spar with me when I first used to go to Spitalfields Market. It turned out he'd got done for bank robbery. I had a lot of time for this man – he was one of those guys you could talk to all day long – and I've seen Sammy since at dos for old boxers (he's retired from the robbery business too now).

It was only when I was writing this book that I found out he'd been both British Flyweight and Lightweight champion in the fifties. In those days he was known as 'Smilin' Sammy' aka 'The Stepney Feather'. He was also the first boxer ever to appear on *This Is Your Life*. You don't want Eamonn Andrews or Michael Aspel bringing you the big red book when you're banged up, do you?

On the day of the hot-pants girls' visit, I said hello to Sammy then waited for the place to quieten down a bit before slipping Charlie-boy a tenner, which was still worth having in the seventies. You folded it up and gave it to them and then the con who does the teas comes along and collects it on the tea-tray. I think they did this on the great old Ronnie Barker show *Porridge* once, so someone must've done their research. I suppose he'd pass it on to Charlie later on, so as to avoid it being found in the search at the end of visiting. I don't know, I ain't been in prison.

The tactic backfired this time, though, because when Granddad saw me do it he got up and said, 'I didn't know you could hand over money here, son.' Then he got out his money to give Charlie-boy a score and the whole place fell about – even the screws were laughing.

The sad end to the Charlie-boy story was that years later he got heavily into drugs and they gave him a life sentence in Mauritius for smuggling heroin, even though I know for a fact it was only for personal use. The British government got him sent back home, so he was a lucky boy really to get banged up here rather than out there. After about five years he was released and started trying to get his life together, but by that time the heroin had got to him to the extent where there was no way back. The heroin had done his lungs, and his other internal organs weren't shaping up too well either. That fucking drug doesn't just mess your brain up, it kills your body as well. We lost Charlie-boy a few years ago, which was a great shame when I think about what a lovely kid he was.

One thing I've noticed while visiting mates who've been banged up over the years is how much the vibe in prisons has changed. On that trip to Maidstone and other visits in the late seventies I always registered how many of the cons would get themselves all smartened up – partly out of pride and partly because you've got your family or friends visiting and you want to look good so people don't worry about you – but as time went on you didn't see that nearly so much. More and more of the prisoners would come slouching in looking like shit, not caring what anyone else thought about them. It was definitely the drug culture that did that. Whether people are just smoking a lot of dope or they're actual skag-heads, that basic pride in yourself seems to be one of the first things to go.

The way my granddad lived his life was the opposite of that. He'd had really bad bronchial problems all his life, and in his later years he had no option but to connect himself up to this great big pump inhaler with a bowl at the bottom – almost like a hubbly-bubbly or some kind of giant home-made bong, only he was using it to stay alive, not to get out of his head. And if you saw him out and about he always looked dapper, however bad he might've been feeling.

You'd never hear him complain. Even the prospect of his own death was contemplated with good-humoured resignation: 'I'm up, son, I'm up' – that was his favourite saying. I really loved my grand-dad, and when he passed on a few years later it was one of the biggest losses I've had in my life. The doctors had told him he was going to die way back when he was just twenty-eight, so he did pretty well to live as long as he did. When he was on his death bed he looked up at me with a broad smile and said, 'I'm eighty-two. They got the numbers the wrong way round.'

CHAPTER 20

THE ALEXANDRA
TAVERN

I'll tell you a good trick for getting the best seat on a plane if you can only afford economy class. Get yourself a cast made and strap it on under your trousers like you've got a broken leg – I was lucky, I had a mate whose mum worked in a hospital so I got her to make it up for me. Then borrow a couple of crutches to hobble onto the plane with, and they'll have to upgrade you somewhere with a bit more legroom. Obviously, your leg's got to be straight, so if there's any seats free in business class they'll put you in there. Otherwise it'll be an aisle or (before they stopped allowing you to sit there) somewhere by the emergency exit.

This might seem like a lot of trouble to go to, not least because you've got to lug the cast around with you for the whole holiday if you want to do the same thing again on the way home, but there was a phase in my life when I did it three or four times in quick succession. OK, so you'll get funny looks if anyone who was on the same flight as you (never mind if it's one of the cabin crew) happens to catch you water-skiing, but that didn't bother me at the time.

The flipside of the masterclass in morality and general manners I was getting from my granddad was an overlapping period of several years – probably from the time I left school onwards – when I was a bit of a scammer. I can see the contradiction between those two things now, but again, at the time it never really bothered me. I suppose in my own mind I was keeping alive the heritage of East End fell-off-the-back-of-a-lorry culture. The docks might've been shutting up shop, but that was no reason the proud tradition of spill-age had to die.

You never looked at yourself as doing anything criminal – at least, I didn't. But from stolen tax discs that would come to you through a dodgy postman, to starting a motor with a screwdriver when it wasn't even technically ours, to the odd bit of sleight of hand with a credit card, there was a fair amount of low-level illegality going on. When you're a teenager who ain't got much money the prospect of living like a king in a hotel for the weekend at someone else's expense can look quite tempting, especially once you're caught up in the dubious mystique of the gentleman conman.

Looking back on all this now, my reaction is, 'Fucking hell, what was I thinking?' Not so much in a moralistic way, although that is part of it, but more in terms of my misplaced confidence that if I got caught I wouldn't go to prison. I did some stupid things at that time which I was lucky not to get done for. OK, I enjoyed some of them, but they were still stupid.

There were a couple of pubs down near where my dad went to school – just north of Victoria Park – where I got away with murders. Not literally murders, but certainly stuff that crossed the thin line that separates a misdemeanour from a felony. It's all getting a bit chi-chi in those parts these days, but both the pubs concerned – the Empress and the Alexandra Tavern – are actually still there (albeit under new management), which is quite unusual given how many East End boozers have gone under over the last few decades. Having so many people coming into the area who are Muslims certainly hasn't helped the area's pub trade, and that's before you even factor in the invasion of the white middle classes.

Now, I don't smoke spliff, and I've never really been able to – it just helicopters me, and I don't really like that feeling. But the air was so thick with it in the Alex in the late seventies that walking in there was like opening curtains. One time we decided we could make the heady atmosphere work for us. I had a mate in those days who had access to a big colour photocopier at his place of work, and I got him to take photographs of a ten-pound note and copy them onto both sides of a piece of paper. They came out a bit grey at first but we fucked about with them for a while and got it as close as it was ever gonna get. In normal daylight you could see the colour wasn't right, but in the kind of brothel-red glow they had at the Alex, with a cloud of marijuana smoke to help you, they could just about pass muster. Bosh! Two drinks and we'll keep the change, thanks – no bother.

We absolutely caned it that night. Obviously, we should've just done it once and moved on somewhere else, but I'm not a great one for relocating. If I'm in a pub I like, I prefer to stay there for the duration. How we avoided getting caught and being sentenced to transportation to Australia for forging the tenners of the realm I will never know, but it must've been a bit of a sickener for the poor sod who had to cash up. And the fact that we never did it again suggested that we knew a destiny as Britain's greatest counterfeiters did not lie ahead of us.

Another time in the Empress we had a load of dodgy lighters that were meant to be Ronsons that we were knocking out for fivers or two quid. I remember a funny little geezer who bought one tried to use it straight away and it set his hair alight. We moved so fast to put him out it must've been like watching Red Adair. Luckily he was OK, but it was another deathblow to the idea of a victimless crime.

I mentioned earlier in this book that there was sometimes an element of hypocrisy about the moral environment I grew up in. This was particularly true when it came to fraud. If you get away with it, you're a lovable rogue, but if someone else does it to you, they're a wanker. The same applies when you get a bit higher up the criminal scale to proper white-collar scams.

People who earn their living on the wrong side of the law tend to see those as their equivalent of getting promoted at work, but the idea that 'it only affects the banks and insurance companies' is total bollocks. I've got as much dislike for the banks and insurance companies as the next man – probably more than most – but anyone can see that's just an excuse, because fraud affects everyone. And when it's focused on an individual victim it can be a terrible thing which absolutely destroys people's lives.

Of course, I didn't see things that way then. In my late teens and early twenties I wouldn't have thought of fraud as something that was really hurting anyone. But luckily before my career as a fraudster could really get off the ground, the movie remake of *Scum* came along to save me from myself. Mary Whitehouse might not have thought that film was a good influence on impressionable young minds, but it certainly worked that way for me. Once you become an actor who might be recognised at any time, you can't really afford to get involved in fraud any more (unless people want to look at your acting and say that it's fraudulent – there's nothing you can do to stop that). So being in a successful film changes your life in that way if no other.

There was no road-to-Damascus moment where someone sold me a dodgy timeshare and I realised it was wrong – apart from anything else, there was no way I would ever buy a timeshare in Damascus. But I do understand the implications of fraud now in a way I didn't as a kid. Everyone seemed to be at it in one form or another when I was growing up. From little things like working cash in hand or dodgy tax discs to the boxes of booze or clothes that would mysteriously appear in people's front rooms around Christmas. This was the grease that made the wheels move. But you only need to go up a gear or two and suddenly those wheels are taking you somewhere you don't really want to go.

If you ask me now if I have any regrets about this, in a way I don't because I learnt from it – as well as earning from it – but on the other hand it's a time in your life that you look back on and think, 'I wasn't a very nice person.' You tell yourself you're not hurting anyone, but you know you are really. I don't know if my parents knew what was going on. I don't suppose my dad would've been too bothered, but then again maybe that was what the whole drama school thing was about. They might've been trying to give me something else to focus on.

I'd like to get one more story from the Empress in before I get onto how the second *Scum* put me back on the straight and narrow. We had some great nights in those pubs, and this one was from a few years earlier – a more innocent time, when I was maybe sixteen or seventeen.

I was seeing a barmaid at the time, and her brother was a big lump who came out of the house once when I'd walked her home. 'What are you doing with my sister?' he demanded, before chasing me off down the road. A few years later I saw him on the TV and recognised him immediately. He wasn't on *Crimewatch*; he was

Tommy, the geezer from *Ground Force* (not Alan Titchmarsh – I don't think I'd have run away if he'd chased me). I met him again a short while after and said, 'You probably won't remember me', to which he replied, 'Oh yes, I do.'

When I was stacking up the fruit and veg for that year in Muswell Hill, I never saw myself being a greengrocer for the rest of my life. Not because there was anything wrong with it as a job, just because the example of what had happened to my dad's shop in Watford had showed me how hard it was getting to compete with the supermarkets. I had no idea what else I'd end up doing. I wasn't really thinking about being an actor any more after *Scum* got banned. So I was lucky to get a break out of the blue which led me down a career path I really enjoyed. I do believe there probably is something like that out there for everyone, but a lot of people just never get the chance to find it.

I was at home at my granddad's one day and happened to answer the phone.

'Hello.'

'Is that Ray?'

'Yeah.'

'We're thinking of making the film *Scum* again.'

'Oh, are you? Well done.'

They asked me if I'd like to do it and told me the fee would be £1,800, so I thought about it for a minute and said, 'OK, alright.' In my mind I still didn't particularly want to be an actor, I just thought of it as work. Then they offered me another film for the same money, which they were going to shoot just before. It was called *That Summer!*, and doing it would mean going down to Torquay and living in a hotel for eight weeks over the summer of 1978. I didn't hesitate so long over that one. I thought, 'Blinding, I can have some mates down – it'll be like a holiday.'

It was like that too, and without me coming home empty-handed and with a sore head like I normally would, either. Not only did
I have a great time down there, I also met my wife-to-be Elaine, and
before I'd even come back to London, she'd already helped me start
to heal the breach with my parents.

That Summer! was a film for young teenagers. You can guess
the kind of thing it was from the title. I was in some kind of
round-the-bay swimming competition and these three Glasgow
sweaties kept having a pop at me so I had to sort them out. The
same people who did *Scum* produced it – Davina Belling and
Clive Parsons – but I wasn't actually meant to be playing the
same character again. I've heard this suggested a few times, but the
film certainly wasn't scripted that way. I probably just acted like
that because I didn't know how to do anything else. I didn't have the
ability to find another character yet, so I just played me every time.

This film is rarely seen these days, although it was shown on TV
late at night in the Granada region once, when someone was kind
enough to make me a copy of it on video. For some reason I got a
BAFTA best newcomer nomination for it, even though I didn't deserve it because I didn't really have the first idea of what I was doing.
Julie Shipley, who played the girl in it, was good, though.

When I eventually went to the BAFTAs, eighteen months or so
later, I knew I wasn't going to be in luck from the moment I got
there. We were sitting way back in the cheap seats, and the iron rule
of award ceremonies is: 'If you ain't down the front, you ain't gonna
win.' Even if you are down the front, you still probably won't win
– they might just have got you there so the cameras can catch the
pissed-off look on your face.

That Summer! didn't win me my first piece of acting silverware,
but it did bring me the ultimate prize, which was my Elaine. She

lived in Manchester at the time, but she was down in Torquay on holiday with her mum and dad and a mate called Carol, who we still see sometimes to this day.

My mate – the actor Tony London, who was in the film with me – went after Elaine at first, but she didn't want to know. I've never really got into competition with friends over women – if that's the way it is, that's the way it is – but I couldn't help holding Elaine's gaze and doing the old puppy-eye thing every now and again. I'd been going out with Julie Shipley for a while, but even though she was a good girl, we weren't really getting along. So me and Elaine met up again on our own the next day and that was that. Tally-ho, chaps, bandits at three o'clock.

Brandy's legacy had served me well. To be honest, I think Elaine had also tapped into it, because she did me with the eye thing too. All of which goes to show that there is such a thing as eyes meeting across a room, and the buzz is even better when you both catch each other looking away and then back at the same time.

Before we met, Elaine had gone to college doing art and design and then got jobs window-dressing for a chain of department stores. But by the time we got together she was working as a Bunny Girl at the Playboy Club in Manchester, although she wasn't wearing her costume when we first met. I soon put paid to that once we got together – I told that bunny costume to hop it.

It's not like Elaine was short of rivals for my attention in Torquay that summer – and the same applied the other way round. All of which made the strength of the instant bond between us even more obvious.

I was certainly a bit of a handful in those days. It was my first time away from home working with a film crew, and it wasn't so much the other actors who were the problem, it was the sparks. This mob were murder – their motto when they went away was 'Drink, fight and fuck' – although obviously they weren't all like that, and I don't want to get anyone in trouble, so if you're still married to one of them, it wasn't him. But the fact that when the film was finally finished I would drive back to London with the electricians rather than my fellow performers shows you who I felt most at home with.

At the end of her holiday Elaine went home with her parents, but pretty much as soon as she got to Manchester I was asking her to come and see me again. She borrowed a car to drive back to Torquay, but she turned the wrong way onto the motorway and headed north instead of south. A psychologist might see this as evidence of her subconscious mind trying to protect her by taking her as far away from me as possible, but really it was the opposite. What made this mistake a good omen was the fact that she carried on driving until she got to Gretna Green, which was where couples used to run off to if they eloped.

When she got there, she asked a policeman if she was 'anywhere near Torquay', and he told her (and feel free to read this in your worst *Braveheart* accent), 'Sorry, love, you're in Gretna Green.' So she turned around and drove all the way back to Devon.

Elaine made it down to Torquay eventually, but obviously her mum was worried as to why it had taken her a whole day. 'Don't you know where the sun goes down?' I enquired respectfully when she finally turned up at my hotel. 'It goes down in the west, babe. So all you've got to do is look at the sun and you might have some idea of where you are.'

A sense of direction has never been my Elaine's strongest suit, but she knows how to put people on the right road when it comes to the things that matter. She was showing this quality already in the first weeks we were together in Torquay. My parents had wanted to make peace for ages but my dad's as stubborn as I am – we were like two rams butting their heads together (and we still are). He wouldn't just say, 'Come home,' he wanted me to ask, but I wasn't having it. So when the two of them made the gesture of bringing my granddad down to Torquay on holiday at the same time as I was working there, that was quite a major concession on their part. I don't think my dad would have come up with that on his own – Mum probably nagged him.

They stayed in a suite at the Imperial Hotel, so they must've been doing alright for money at the time. And Elaine was with me when I got the call to tell me that they were there, so she came along too to have dinner at the hotel. Things could still have gone either way at that stage, as I hadn't seen much of them over the last eighteen months or so, and there were still issues that needed to be sorted out. But it was all kind of cool – Elaine met 'em and then she danced with my granddad, and by the time we parted company at the end of the night, we were all on friendly terms and she'd made a really good impression on them.

It went so well that before *That Summer!* was even finished I'd hired a car to drive her back to London to see them all again. There's a big street in Winchmore Hill near where our house was that all the rich people used to live on. It was sort of like a lower-key version of Bishop's Avenue, just off the North Circular, where all the millionaires have mansions that are going to rack and ruin because they never get around to actually living in them.

I turned down this road saying, 'Nearly there, babe', and I could see the pound-note signs lighting up in Elaine's eyes. Once I'd taken it that far I thought, 'I've got to follow through with this', so I pulled into one of the driveways and went up and knocked on the door. An old boy came out who she probably thought was the butler, so

I spun him a line about being lost or some other bollocks and went back to the car. She'd got out of the passenger seat by that time and was looking a bit confused. Luckily I was able to put her mind at rest by telling her, 'I fucking had you there, didn't I? You thought we were cake-o bake-o!'

She still married me within about a year of seeing where I actually lived, though. So she can't have been in it for the money, which subsequent events would confirm was definitely for the best.

CHAPTER 21

THE TATE & LYLE SUGAR FACTORY, SILVERTOWN

There was one thing I came back from Torquay with that I could've done without, and that was a charge of marijuana possession for a bit of wacky baccy that wasn't even mine. One night I had a party in my room in the Grand Hotel – just for a few of the boys in the crew. Unfortunately, there were two of the make-up women staying downstairs who were not very nice. I usually get on really well with the make-up girls, but I didn't with these two – not in a nasty way, I just didn't have 'em in the company because they were horrible gossips.

Anyway, I had this party, and they complained about the noise. Maybe they were just pissed off that they hadn't been invited, I don't know. Either way, that was fair enough. The bad part was that they told the concierge I had drugs in the room – which I didn't because that's not my game. So I came back from the set the next day to be met by a police detective who had already been in there (which I thought was a fucking liberty, but obviously I don't own the room, the hotel does).

He told me they'd found a small quantity of marijuana. I said, 'It ain't mine – you can give me a drugs test if you like', but that didn't stop them taking me down the station. I knew who it belonged to – a mate of mine who did like a smoke – but just because he'd dropped me in it with some grass didn't mean I had to become one. Maybe he should've come forward and held his hands up, but he didn't. The whole thing was a bigger deal then legally than it would be now, but my main concern was that I didn't want my dad thinking I was on drugs – especially when I wasn't. Relations with my parents were just starting to get back on track, and this was the first time I'd been away working on a film, so I didn't want them thinking I was on the slippery slope to reefer madness.

When I went back to Torquay to appear in court in December of 1978 I decided to plead guilty. I'd been brought up never to do that, but in this case there was fuck all else I could do. I just wanted this one out of the way with nothing in the papers to upset the family.

Not long before my court appearance, the producers Davina and Clive phoned me up and said, 'Since you're going back, anyway, could we do some pick-up shots?' They'd been really good about sorting out the legal side of things, so I couldn't say no. Next thing I knew I had to swim out into Torquay bay in the middle of winter, which was a bonus – especially when my ankle got snagged by a fishing hook that dragged me under the sea. I just about managed to pull the hook out of my leg and get home in one piece. Then I got found guilty and paid the fine without my Old Man finding out, so that was more good news.

Fast-forward thirty-five years, and having this conviction on my record still causes me problems getting into America. Every time I go there, which I do a lot, I get pulled out of the line and have to sit in a room and be investigated (not intimately, but it's still a pain in the arse). When you get off a plane after an eleven-hour flight the last thing you want to do is spend another four hours being asked pointless questions in a brightly lit room, especially when you're a smoker like I am. And all because someone who was a mate of yours – bless him – smoked a joint in your hotel room and left a bit of gear there. The worst thing is that at the end of the interrogation they always say, 'You shouldn't have to come here any more, this will clear off your record now', but it never does. I always tell them, 'You say that every time.'

I often see Frank Roddam when I'm on those flights back and forth to LA, either that or hanging about in the Chateau Marmont. He's the guy who got me to be a rocker in *Quadrophenia* between the two films for Belling and Parsons, and he's still got those little-boy looks he always had – I suppose the millions he must've earned for inventing *Masterchef* can't have done any harm in that area.

I wish he'd let me have a haircut like his in *Quadrophenia*, instead of sending round Danny La Rue to give me Liberace's old barnet. I was happy to pay tribute to my childhood memories of mods and rockers roaring through Plaistow, and I didn't even mind sharing a bath with the lovely Phil Daniels, although I'd have rather not done it with hair that looked like it'd just got back from a three-month residency in Vegas.

The funny thing about my performances in the two films I did with Phil at that time – *Quadrophenia* and *Scum* – is that I wasn't either capable or interested enough to have a say in how I looked on the screen yet. I didn't realise I could have a say in the development of the character – I just turned up, listened to what the director had to say and did the lines as best I could. If I'd played those parts a few years later I would have done them very differently, but they might not have turned out nearly so well, because how little I knew about what I was doing probably fed into the rawness of the characters.

A lot of the Anna Scher boys were in both films too, and they knew the ropes a lot better than I did. They were winding me up a bit on *Quadrophenia*. One of them (not Phil) came up behind me in a dressing room and said, ''Ere, Ray, I'm doing your part in *Scum*.' I just held his gaze in the mirror and said, 'Oh, are you mate? Well, good luck to ya.' I knew he was digging me out. You do get tested in those situations, especially when you've got a load of young fellas together.

When the time came to do the scene in the alley at Shepherd's Bush Market where they're chasing me on the bikes, the guy who was needling me about *Scum* was meant to be the first one off and at me. Peter Brayham, who was the stuntman and a great mate of mine, told me what I had to do, which was basically crash into the boxes. I'm not that great on a bike, but all I had in my head was 'he's the first one off'.

After I'd crashed the bike, I was supposed to stay there while they all piled into me. Instead, I jumped up and chinned him. All the stunties were going, 'Stop! Stop!' but they couldn't get there in time to stop me giving him a good larrapping. The geezer didn't bear a grudge afterwards. I think he respected me for it, because he knew he'd been out of order. Either way, we're still mates a quarter of a century later.

When you're doing these films – the second *Scum* was the same – you don't know whether they're going to end up being any good or not. One of the things I was beginning to learn at this time was that the scenes which work the best tend to be the ones that are done in a very simple way. The billiard-balls scene in *Scum* was a good example.

Phil Mayhew, who was on the camera, did hand-held all the way while I walked down the stairs, took a sock out of my pocket to put the billiard balls in and then hit poor old Phyllis over the head with 'em. Because subconsciously you know there's not been a cut, even people watching with no interest in how films are made think, 'How the fuck did he hit Phil over the head and not kill him?' I think Phil was thinking that too.

Here's how we did it: there was a geezer lying on the floor by the door who swapped the sock with the balls for another one – containing ping pong balls in *papier-mâché* – as I walk in. We still have to have some weight in it so you can see I ain't giving Phil a chance when he turns round and I go whack. It's the shock of it that makes it effective.

I've not said too much about the technical side of things in this book, because I've found that the more I've learnt about those aspects of film-making, the less I enjoy actually watching a movie. And I don't want to put you lot through the same pain I've suffered. One thing I do think is that we don't give audiences enough credit for being willing to be challenged by something real. I remember when Hollywood made a more commercial version of *Scum* called *Bad Boys* – with Sean Penn in it – they swapped the billiard balls in a sock for a pillow-case full of Coca-Cola cans. I suppose there might've been a bit of product placement going on there, but I don't think it was very credible.

By the time we got to the second *Scum*, Alan Clarke was manipulating us quite mercilessly to get the level of realism he wanted. When it came to the race riot in the borstal hall he went up to all the black kids and said, 'Listen, all the white guys are going to have a go at you here.' Then he told the rest of us to 'watch the black kids – they might be gonna stick it on ya'. They were alright that lot – I think they'd come out of a youth club in Leytonstone – but they were definitely there to do a job, and there was never much doubt about what was going to happen as soon as someone said, 'Action!'

I remember saying to Francis – who played Baldy, the black guy I use the tool on in the film – 'Are you with them or with us?' When he said the latter I thought, 'Thank God for that! He's a second dan karate expert.' It was actually Phil Daniels who saved me from getting a belting in that scene. One fella came at me and as I chinned him he grabbed my legs and pulled me down on the floor. They were all piling in on top when Phil pulled me up and got me out of there, laying about him all the while. That's one of the things I love about Phil – he's a game little fucker who takes no prisoners, especially when he's got some red wine inside him.

I'd had my last little go at the boxing by then. After a couple of years away I'd found that I missed it and wanted to get back in the ring. As comebacks go, mine went better than Ricky Hatton's but not as well as George Foreman's. Having left the Repton I trained at the Black Lion in West Ham, an excellent boxing gym with a blinding pub attached. My first fight was in the old Territorial Army place on the side of West Ham Park. I got off to a good start but I wasn't fully fit yet, so I ran out of steam halfway through the second round. I tried to batten down the hatches as I was probably ahead at that stage, but it was too long to last and I lost on points.

You think you'll be a bit wiser two years on and your mind will be working better, but I found I'd lost some of that speed I'd had before. There's a natural kind of fitness you have in your late teens – especially if you're not drinking too much yet – which gets much harder to maintain by the time you're in your early twenties, so I wasn't in much better shape by the time I got to the second fight.

That was in the old Tate & Lyle sugar factory, the big white building in Silvertown. I think they were renting it out for events to try and make a bit of money, because the docks had more or less gone by then. The night in question was a West Ham boxing club show and I fought a guy called Chris Christiansen – not Kris Kristofferson, he'd have been singing.

Chris was a pretty solid performer who went on to win the Southern area title, but by now I was a bit less ring-rusty so I just about managed to pull through. I still wasn't fully fit, so I had to hold him a lot in the last round – I needed something to lean on by then, anyway. I know Chris didn't think I'd won it, but he had a head as big as Bournemouth and I couldn't miss it. Either way, once I'd staggered out of the ring at the end of that fight I knew the game was up. As soon as I won, I retired.

Stanley Kubrick used some of the old warehouses up that way to film his Vietnam movie *Full Metal Jacket* a few years later. The funny thing about that was that we always used to know Dagenham as 'The 'Nam', anyway, so a war story about a bad night down there – which there were plenty of, as that place was almost as bad as Beirut – was always a 'Nam flashback.

That last fight was it for me as far as boxing was concerned. Although I still enjoyed socialising with people from the fight game, the only time I put my gloves on again was for a long boxing se- quence in the ITV series *Fox*, which I'll come back to a bit later on. Once I was with Elaine I didn't need to get in the ring to take a bit of punishment any more, anyway. All I had to do was come home late. And when she'd come for me with those verbal volleys, there was no time to put my head-guard on.

Not long after *Scum* was finished, I got a last-minute call from the producers saying the film was being shown in Cannes and they needed me and Alan out there quick. They couldn't get us on a normal flight, so they'd chartered a little three-seater to get us from Gatwick to Nice.

We must've looked a right odd couple on that runway. I know what I was wearing, because I recently found a photo taken just before I left. I was modelling a smart college-boy look with a crisp pair of cream Sta-Prest, brown brogues, a pale green linen shirt and a Pringle-type jumper, topped off with some nice blond highlights in my hair (well, it was nearly the eighties). By way of contrast, Alan was probably the unsmartest man in the world. I had a great time with him, but he wouldn't know how to put a bit of clobber on if you paid him.

On that occasion he was wearing cowboy boots and three-quarter-length flared jeans with a crusty roll-neck jumper, and a velvet jacket with a little tear at the back. His hair was all curly and it didn't look like it'd seen a comb in a while, never mind a blond highlight. Factor in our very different accents – his Scouse and my London – and it was obvious we weren't brothers.

Alan never gave a fuck about money or success. After *Scum* he got offered six movies out in LA, including *The Omen II*. He was sitting in a shed down the bottom of someone's garden out there, trying to work out what to do, then he just said, 'I can't have this', and came home. He shunned Hollywood to make the documentary-type films that he really believed in back in the UK instead. All power to the man – he was another Ken Loach as far as I was concerned.

Alan was ill at the time of that Cannes trip. He had yellow jaundice, and probably shouldn't have been leaving the house, let alone getting in a very small plane. I love flying now and I've been up in Spitfires and Mosquitoes since, but at that stage the idea of strapping myself into a metal coffin was quite new to me, and it was hard not to be struck by how fucking tiny that plane was.

The weather wasn't looking too clever either. And as we were standing around waiting to get introduced to the pilot in the VIP bit of Gatwick, it was all starting to feel a little bit Buddy Holly. I remember thinking, 'I don't want this plane to go down now I've just cracked it.' Living fast and dying young worked alright for James Dean, but that's no reason for me to be doing it.

At that point the captain came out to meet us and I was reassured by the fact that he had the biggest moustache I'd ever seen – a proper old RAF handlebar, like a rear-gunner in a Lancaster would've had. So we got on the plane, with me and Clarkey in the two seats at the back and him at the controls in the front. The take-off was OK, but once you're properly flying in one of those little planes you feel yourself dropping out of the sky every time you hit an air pocket.

It was a three-and-a-half-hour flight. At times it felt like it would've been quicker to go by car as the pilot negotiated his way around a series of storms. About halfway through, Clarkey leant forward – don't forget he's got yellow jaundice – and said to the captain (and you've got to read this to yourself in a really strong Scouse accent to get the full picture), 'Eh, Captain, you know, could you drop down a couple of thousand feet so I can have a piss out of the window?' Understandably, the captain's not having that, so I give Clarkey the sick bag and say, 'Do it in that, Al.'

Now he's got to stand up to take a piss, but the problem is the plane is too cramped for him to do that, so he ends up all bent over. He whacks his cock out into the sick bag and pees into it. I've got to say that the smell from the yellow jaundice is diabolical. I'm gagging, the captain's moustache has drooped, but Clarkey's feeling very relieved. Finally we come into Nice airport and the captain taxis the plane round the runway. At this point he's supposed to see us off and show us where to go, but instead he just opens the door and runs away. He's had enough of us, so he's just fucked off.

Me and Clarkey haven't got a clue what to do, so we're just wandering around on the runway – if that happened now you'd probably get shot. Eventually we find our way into the terminal, and at this point it suddenly dawns on me that we've left Alan's piss in the sick bag on the floor of the plane. When that pilot gets back onboard for the return flight, he's in for a nasty surprise.

Once we finally made it to Cannes, our accommodation went up a couple of notches. We were staying on Don Boyd's boat. Don was the overall producer of the film – who'd just got Clive and Davina in to do the donkey work – and this was the first of several great trips abroad he took me on. Don was someone I had a lot of time for. He's one of those big figures in the British film industry – like Jeremy Thomas who I ended up doing *Sexy Beast* with – without whom very little would ever actually happen.

It was very exciting being at Cannes for the first time. After what happened with the TV version being banned, the idea of the second *Scum* even being shown in a cinema seemed very unlikely to me. Now all of a sudden I was in this mad glamorous world with the Palme d'Or and all that stuff going on. There were film stars everywhere – I was the only one I didn't know.

Alan Clarke was the perfect person to share that experience with, because however much of an outsider I thought I was, I could never be as much of one as him. That didn't stop him making the most of his opportunities, though. Fuck me, that man loved a bird, and they were still attracted to him, despite what he looked like.

Clarkey could talk to anyone, he just had that way about him. I remember the film I really loved which was out at the time was a vampire comedy called *Love at First Bite*. The first time I saw it (in Margate with Elaine when I was filming *Fox*) I was laughing so much it made me cry. So you can imagine how excited I was when

I saw the star of it, George Hamilton, standing outside the Carlton Hotel in all his Transylvanian gear and the make-up and everything. I pointed him out to Alan, who must've smiled at him as he walked up the steps, because George Hamilton – thinking that he knew him, even though they'd never met before – said, 'Hello, how are you?'

Actors in those situations usually pretend they know everyone, because otherwise they get too stressed out trying to remember whether they actually do or not. Alan would've known this and was happy to take advantage of it, so he was standing there with George Hamilton going, ''Ow's the kids?' And then they got into some big debate about something. That was what the whole week was like, and even though I've been back to Cannes on a bigger budget a few times since, you never forget your first time. Especially not if Clarkey's involved.

CHAPTER 22

HACKNEY MARSHES

In between my first brushes with the international jet set, I was still doing the same kind of things I'd always done, like trying to stay out of strife at the Charleston or the Two Puddings in Stratford, or playing Sunday football on Hackney Marshes. As a consequence of going to school in Enfield, I'd had to play a lot of my football in alien territory, where people's skill and understanding of the game were frankly not up to the level I had been raised to expect. But once I was a bit older and back in East London, I was finally in a position to put that right.

Hackney Marshes was the place I liked to play best. It's amazing the way the pitches stretch out into the distance, and if you're one of those East Enders who doesn't leave your manor too much, that might be one of the biggest open spaces you ever get to know. You can't let the sense of freedom go to your head, though – you have to keep your wits about you. I remember playing there once when a car drove onto the pitch next to us and tried to run one of the players over. Maybe England might have more of a chance at the World Cup if we were allowed to do that. Either way, there were a few shooters flying about that day on the Marshes. A couple of the games stopped to watch, but it was the ones which carried on as if this was a per-fectly normal everyday occurrence that made the biggest impression.

I'd like to be able to say that at the time I was taking a similar-ly level-headed approach to how well things seemed to be going with what was now officially my acting career. Unfortunately, that wouldn't be true. I didn't carry on being the same no-nonsense down-to-earth geezer I'd always been. When I saw myself in the finished version of *Scum* – more or less holding my own with a lot of much more experienced and technically gifted actors – I didn't think about how much I still had to learn, I decided I was Jack the fucking Biscuit.

Going to America with Don Boyd probably didn't help in that regard. Because *Scum* was kind of the big underground film at the time, my first trip to New York found me moving in very different circles to the ones I was used to. Don took me to the Mudd Club, which was full of all these fucking strange people. Siouxsie from Siouxsie and the Banshees was there being 'punk' – which seemed to be a bit of a pose where everyone had to look really solemn and try to fuck everyone else off. She seemed like a bit of a prat to me at the time but I'm sure she was just doing her thing.

Siouxsie's wasn't the only famous face to come looming up out of the dry ice in that place. Yoko Ono was floating about too, as was Andy Warhol . . . hole . . . hole. I didn't know too much about all these arty types, but I went up to him and said, 'Alright, how are you going?' He said hello back politely enough, so as far as I was concerned he was one of the good ones.

It's at about this time that I take a hit on something that is prob-ably angel dust and start to notice that the waitresses are all the most beautiful women you'd ever see. But after a few 'Hello, darlin''s my eyes start to adjust to the light properly, and now I'm thinking,

'Woah, fuck me! Something ain't right here – the old Adam's apples are a bit prominent. These birds are all geezers. You could make a mistake here!'

By now the angel dust is properly taking hold and I'm not used to this kind of feeling. To be honest, I'm properly shitting myself, so I'm working my way around the outside wall like a kid who can't swim hanging onto the edge of the pool. Eventually I get to the exit and promptly fall all the way down the stairs. So I get in a cab and ask the guy to take me to the Gramercy Park Hotel and he goes, 'Well, I ain't gonna take you to California am I, bud?' When I finally get back to the hotel, Don Boyd's standing there looking at his watch going, 'Raymond, you were twenty-five minutes longer than I expected you to be.'

It was a great way to see New York for the first time because I was going in through the underbelly – not the gangsters but the artists and bohemians. I still had a massive chip on my shoulder, though, so I probably didn't make the best impression.

Before one screening I remember being introduced to Richard Gere, who was one of the biggest stars in the world at the time, and he totally blanked me. I can understand why now – after all, he didn't know me from Adam Ant – but at the time I remember thinking, 'Fuck you, that ain't very nice, is it?'

After we'd all sat there and watched the film, Richard came up to us again. I think Don Boyd probably knew him because he said, 'Ray, invite Richard to the party after.' But I said, 'No, Richard's very busy. Ain't you, Richard? He's definitely too busy to come to the party.' Richard Gere's probably a nice guy who has to talk to a million people a day – why should he have any idea who I am? – but that was my attitude at the time. I was quite fuck-you about everything. So maybe I had a bit more in common with Siouxsie than I thought I did.

When I eventually got to the party, they fitted me up with this starlet who became quite a famous actress later on. I'm just talking normally to this reporter from *Hollywood Tonight* and all of a sudden this bird has been slipped onto my arm. It ain't her fault they're trying to pair us up like Beauty and the Beast – she's been told to do it, which they used to do years ago, and I suppose they still do today. It's good for you to be seen with a starlet, and good for them to get their face out there, but all the time I'm thinking, 'My fiancée's at home – how's she gonna react if she sees this?'

I'd rather not say who the unlucky lady was – not because she had anything to be embarrassed about, but because I did, as she was a lovely girl and under other circumstances, yeah ... Oh, alright then, it was Jane Seymour, and I ended up being quite rude to her. I've done enough things I've had to apologise for over the years not to have to make up imaginary misdeeds. So I don't see why I'd have a painful memory of telling the future *Dr Quinn Medicine Woman*, 'This is my film – it's nothing to do with you, love', if I hadn't actually done it. That's just one step away from 'Don't you know who I am?' really, though, isn't it?

The problem with thinking you've cracked it is it's all too easy to get complacent and piss the whole thing up the wall. I'd come out of shooting *Scum* and gone straight into *Fox*. It was a thirteen-part ITV drama series about a big South London family. They weren't so much gangsters, more a strong, old-fashioned family who looked after each other in a way that was becoming less and less common then, but which I still believe in today. Maybe that was why it struck quite a chord with people at the time, even though not many people remember it now.

It was while I was doing *Fox* that the hype really started for the cinema release of *Scum*. I remember watching it come on Barry

Norman's *Film 79* with some of the other actors in *Fox* – Peter Vaughan from *Citizen Smith* and Larry Lamb, who was on *EastEnders* for a long time years later, were definitely there. You could tell something big was happening, but I ended up being quite distanced from it all, because I'd chosen the two weeks leading up to the London opening to get married to Elaine and go on our honeymoon in Lanzarote.

Once we landed back in London, we got off the plane and straight into a cab to the premiere at the Prince Charles just off Leicester Square. There was quite a lot of hysteria and people fainting in the cinema (which I'm sure was a rent-a-crowd Don Boyd had paid for. Why not? They'd do it in America. That's why I love Don to death, because he'd set that kind of thing up – even though he never admitted to me that he had). I remember thinking, 'Fucking hell! I had no idea this was going to be such a big deal.' It was probably a good thing I didn't, because I'd already lost enough of whatever discipline I'd managed to accumulate as an actor.

I remember one of the producers of *Fox* telling me something that got me quite annoyed at the time. 'You're doing alright, Ray,' he said. 'But there's nothing going on in your eyes.' Looking back now, I can see that what made me angry about this remark was the fact that it was absolutely bang on. It took me a couple of years to get over the initial shock of someone digging me out like that, but as time went on I began to realise that just because you were saying the right words and making the right movements, that didn't mean there was anything actually behind them.

I'm not sure exactly how I eventually managed to make a deeper connection between who I was and what I was doing as an actor. Maybe it was getting a bit more life experience. Maybe it was having a few disappointments. Maybe it was losing some people who

I loved. But I don't think I'd ever have been able to do it without Elaine at my side.

People have sometimes said to me that it was a strange time to get married – just as my career was taking off. But it's not a choice I've ever regretted, in fact quite the reverse. I wasn't one of those people who needed showbiz to get a bird. I'd done all that by then, and I needed someone around who was a strong enough character to stand up to me when I was getting a bit full of myself. My Elaine didn't just do personal guidance. On the next job I got after *Scum*, she gave me the most important bit of professional advice I've ever received.

If the people making the film had got their way, Elaine wouldn't even have been around to save the day. We'd only just got married when I was offered the lead role in an American film called *Ladies and Gentlemen, The Fabulous Stains*. Well, that wasn't the original title. At first it was called *All Washed Up*, but I think they changed that title because they were worried it was going to become a self-fulfilling prophecy (which, in a way, it did).

It was a funny old script about a load of punk rockers on a tour bus, which was going to be directed by an old hippie and self-confessed mate of Roman Polanski's called Lou Adler. They'd cast some big old characters to be in such a confined space, but we'll come to them in a minute.

When they asked me to do it off the back of *Scum* I said, 'OK, fine', but only if I could bring my wife with me. They didn't fancy that too much but I said, 'Listen, I've just got married and I want to stay that way, so either my wife comes with me, or I don't come at all.' Neither Elaine nor I have ever been the jealous type – that's part of the reason we've stuck together so long – and these days when I go away for work she's probably glad to get rid of me. But at the time we'd only just got hitched, and I didn't want to be out in Vancouver for a big chunk of 1980 without her.

It was a good job I felt that way. Because when I was trying to get my head around the idea of playing a character who was the lead singer in a band, I didn't have the first fucking clue of how I was going to do it. Singing a song I could do, but the idea of me becoming a rock star and putting on some kind of performance just seemed completely impossible.

It was Elaine who told me something which now looks embarrassingly obvious written down, but that was all the more reason why I needed to hear it. She said, 'But you're not a singer, are you? You're an actor . . . so act it!' I realise how ridiculous this sounds, but that's when the penny dropped for me. 'Oh, so you've got to make out to be something else other than what you are, and make it look real. I get it now.' I must have been driving her mad. When it comes to how I'd managed to get through a couple of years of drama college and lead roles in two versions of *Scum* without somehow waking up and smelling that particular cup of coffee, your guess is as good as mine.

The message had got through just in time, because when it came to looking comfortable onstage, I was about to face a pretty searching examination. The other three members of my band were going to be Steve Jones and Paul Cook of the Sex Pistols and Paul Simonon of The Clash, all of whom had a certain amount of experience in that area.

There was a fair bit of tension around our first meeting. As I've said before, I'd enjoyed the Sex Pistols' music, but a bunch of fucking geezers who picked their nose and spat at people? I ain't gonna like them very much, am I? What made it worse was I'd had a couple of run-ins with Johnny Rotten at the auditions for *Quadrophenia*, where he was up for Phil's role as Jimmy (Jimmy Pursey had a go at that one too – I think Frank Roddam was aiming for the punk audience at that point). He's funny, John, and he's a bit of an intellectual on the quiet, but he's one of those people that if you ask him a question, he'll answer it with another one.

That type is all very well in real life, so long as you don't have to live with them, but they're a nightmare to do acting improvisations with. John's probably grown up a bit now – or maybe he hasn't, it's hard to tell from the butter adverts – but the concept of two people working together for the benefit of the piece was not something he could really get his head round at the time. It was all about him being Johnny Rotten.

To be honest I thought he was a bit of a cunt, and when I got the hump with him, he didn't like it. But if I was expecting things to go the same way when I met Jonesy and the two Pauls, I'd got it completely wrong. I actually loved them, and we're all still mates to this day. Jonesy's still a live wire now. I was on his radio show in LA a while back, and we kept talking in rude cockney rhyming slang that no one else in the studio understood, so you can see how much we've matured.

Looking back at that film now, I'm quite happy with the singing, and the bits where I beat up a couple of rock stars – Fee Waybill of The Tubes and a new-wave guy called Black Randy (who wasn't actually black) – it's the stuff in between that's the problem. I was making progress, but the odd line is still a bit slow and some of my acting's a bit naff.

Diane Lane played the girl who ends up turning into a kind of prototype Lady Gaga in the film. She was only fifteen or sixteen at the time, but she ran rings round me, which worked well on screen as the story needed her to be fucking me over left, right and centre, anyway. I didn't mind playing second fiddle to her because she was a tremendous actress then and she still is.

The same is true of Laura Dern, who plays her sister in it. They were both a bit young to be in a film where there was an element of nudity involved, to be honest, and there was something a bit sleazy about the way it was being directed. Diane had her version of my dad's 'Give up while you're in front' moment at the premiere, when someone in her family asked her, 'What about that film was worth your arse?'

I kind of agreed with that verdict, to be honest. But after Paramount effectively shelved the movie for some complicated tax reason that I didn't understand, its reputation started to grow, to the point where it's now considered a 'cult classic' by a lot of people who haven't actually seen it. The saying 'absence makes the heart grow fonder' is as true in the cinema as it is anywhere else. As my experiences with the first *Scum* and now *Ladies And Gentlemen, The Fabulous Stains* proved, sometimes the best thing that can happen to you as an actor is to be quite shit in a film and then have it not come out.

Getting no work and having to receive secret food parcels off your mother-in-law is not quite such a good look. But that's how things worked out for me in the first couple of years after Elaine and I got married. After the success of *Scum* and *Quadrophenia* I'd thought, 'This acting lark's a doddle.' But once we got back from America, the phone suddenly stopped ringing.

I probably didn't do myself any favours by moving up north and buying a house in Stockport, but that was where Elaine's family lived, and it's important for a woman to be near her mother after she's got married. Well, maybe not for all women, but certainly for this one.

We'd tried living in London together for a while before we got married. My mum wouldn't let Elaine stay overnight in Church

Street until we were officially man and wife, so we moved out into a flat above a launderette in White Hart Lane. You didn't need any heaters in the winter because of the warmth from the machines, but in the summer it was unbearable. I was trying to do the place up a bit to make it nicer for her, so I got my cousin Charlie-boy round to help. Let's just say the two of us going into business together as handymen if and when the acting work dried up was probably not an option.

Charlie was in between prison sentences at the time and he brought over this nail-gun he had to help me put up a curtain rail. We should've been drilling holes and putting rawlplugs in, but instead we were just nailing this fucking thing into the concrete walls. At one point the gun jammed, and he was bracing it against the floor to free it when it shot a nail down through the launderette's ceiling. It was like a cartoon – this round hole appeared in the floor and we were stood above it doing a double take. Then we looked down through the hole and saw a woman sitting there with a laundry bag.

We ran down the stairs and to the front of the shop to check she was alright. There was the woman sitting perfectly contentedly reading a magazine, and there was her laundry bag next to her – nailed to the fucking floor. It frightened the life out of us because that nail could've gone straight through her head.

I was working on *Fox* at this time, so we were doing OK for money, but I was away on set a lot and probably not quite adjusted to the discipline of paying rent yet, so I must've missed the odd week here and there. One day, the big burly geezer who owned the launderette came round when I was out. He said, 'Tell your Old Man to sort this out', but Elaine ain't telling me because she knows there'll be murders. So, a few days later he comes back, and this time he's really pushing his luck.

While he's popped into the shop downstairs, Elaine phones up my dad and says, 'This fella keeps coming round.' Within ten minutes he's down the A10. All she's heard is his car pull up and the next thing she knows my dad's dragged the guy out of the launderette and is smashing his head against his car door. We lived there for another six months without paying rent after that, which seems a bit wrong of us in hindsight, but needs must when you're young and making your way. And on Elaine's part you'd probably have to classify this incident under 'Welcome to the family'.

CHAPTER 23

THE CORNER OF WELL STREET AND MARE STREET

Elaine and I had our wedding reception in the Belgrave Hotel in Reddish, near Stockport. Her family are Irish, and I was a bit worried about bringing the London mob, the Manchester mob and the Irish mob together. Especially as Mountbatten had just got blown up on his fishing boat. I remember thinking, 'It'll be just my luck if one of those that've come from over the water decides to make a joke about Lord Louis' plimsolls floating past and the whole place goes up like a tinderbox.'

Luckily, on the day it all went off surprisingly smoothly, in fact it was a fantastic occasion. The mums got on well – I think that was the key to it. There had been a bit of an incident the night before when the guy running the hotel got the hump about the noise in the early hours and shut the bar. I was safely tucked up in bed by then to be at my best for the big op in the morning, but by all accounts my cousin Charlie-boy got a jemmy out of his car and cleared the optics, so there were murders over that the next day. They didn't know how lucky they were though – at least he hadn't brought his nail-gun and tried to do some DIY for 'em.

We didn't have a lot of money to spend on it, but that night was one of the best parties I've ever been to. We had about 250 people and not a black eye or a freshly broken nose between them. When it was over, Elaine and I fucked off on honeymoon and came back to *Scum*. Then by the time we were in Canada for *Ladies and Gentlemen, The Fabulous Stains* a few months later – watching Roberto Durán beat Sugar Ray Leonard on TV, live from Montreal – we'd bought a house in Bredbury, Stockport, for twenty-eight grand.

This was where the food parcels from Elaine's mum came in. When we'd got married, I'd been quite old-fashioned about it, saying, 'You don't need to work no more, I'll look after you.' But it turned out that promise was much easier to make than it was to keep. The buzz around *Scum* having evaporated so quickly, and all of a sudden being 200 miles from home meant that there was very little prospect of getting any work.

I had no choice but to sign on, which I didn't like doing, but fuck me it was hard up there at that time. The mills had all just shut down and the unemployment was unbelievable – way worse than down south. If I'd been a Mancunian I could maybe have got more acting work, but they didn't need another Londoner in *Coronation Street*, because they already had Mike Baldwin aka Johnny Briggs.

The one positive thing about the whole situation for me – and I did have some great times up there – was in terms of my understanding of people. Without even realising it I had probably been raised to believe in a clear dividing line at Watford Gap services, where the Northerners started, but all I could see when I lived up there in the early eighties was a lot of really hard-working people who were having the choice to go to work taken away from them.

Everyone wanted to be a cab driver, because if you're a normal guy who is lucky enough to still have a car, that is the one job you can give yourself without anyone else's say-so. The only problem was how many cabbies could Manchester sustain? Especially when there was hardly any trade because no one could afford to get a cab.

In professional terms at that time in my life I couldn't get arrested. But off-screen it seemed I got arrested all too easily. For someone with a quick temper like mine, the possibility that someone might recognise you – which had become a fact of life after the second *Scum* came out – can make day-to-day life a lot more complicated. I was walking through the West End down in London one day, when I saw a security guy I knew outside Bobby's Bar at the back of the Café Royal. I asked him what he was doing there and he said, 'I'm looking after James Cagney – he's inside talking to someone.'

Cagney was one of my all-time favourite actors, so I decided to hang about for a while in the hope of saying hello to him when he came out of the bar. After about half an hour I had to go, so as not to be late for a meeting with an agent, but the bodyguard said he was going to be a while yet, so I decided to come back later. If I hadn't made that decision I'd have been on the tube and gone in forty minutes' time, instead of stepping off the kerb to cross Piccadilly on the way back to the Café Royal at the exact moment one of those motorcycle despatch riders decided to run a red light.

He sees me step out, but instead of braking he revs up and comes at me even faster. I have to step back quickly to stop myself getting run over. Obviously I've called him a cunt or whatever under my breath and he's heard me – I don't know how through his helmet – and stopped his bike to have a row. But where he's slammed on the brakes too suddenly he's turned the front wheel and fallen off his bike onto the bonnet of a parked car. It's not just me laughing at him now, it's everyone at the crossing, and this doesn't seem to have improved his mood, because now he's charging at me like a lunatic.

I'm all done up smart for my meeting in a new cream Mac and I'm on my way to meet Jimmy Cagney, so I am not interested in this geezer. But he's still tearing towards me with his head down and his crash-helmet on, so I give him a bit of a barrage – bang, bang, bang – on the visor, but it's still hurt him, and as I've upped him for what I thought was going to be the last time, his crash-helmet's come off. At this point I'm seeing his biker's earring with a cross in it and thinking, 'Now you're in trouble, mate', so I give him a proper larrapping.

I don't want to get nicked, so I've got to have it away sharpish, which should be easy enough because there are thousands of people around. Unfortunately, a high proportion of those people suddenly seem to be wearing police uniforms. I don't know how or why this has happened, but the Old Bill are coming at me from all sides. It's as if a gate has opened in the Statue of Eros's arsehole and they've all piled out, waving their truncheons like the *Keystone Cops*.

At this crucial moment, some brain surgeon standing by the railings shouts out, 'It's the fella off of *Scum*!' I give him a look as if to say, 'Much obliged, mate – thank you very much.' The police have got me in the long run now even if I do get away, which I don't, because I am thoroughly nicked.

The Old Bill take me away to the station round the back of Savile Row, and by the time I get there I can hear the other geezer shouting and screaming. They've pulled him 'cos I've said that he attacked me – counter-charge, and in any case it's true. Once the police have got you for something, it's best not to make a fuss – there's no point turning them any further against you.

Me and the biker had to go to court together at Bow Street magistrates court, which used to be just off Covent Garden, which isn't there any more. We both said our piece and I ended up getting found guilty, which wasn't really fair because he did attack me first, but because the police dragged me away I didn't get a chance to find myself any witnesses.

I was fined £120, which normally I'd delay paying as long as possible – 'I'd like time, please, your honour', that's how you put it off – but on this occasion I just said, 'I'll give you a cheque now.' The despatch rider – horrible geezer he was, totally in the wrong – was there too, so as I walked past him I said, 'It was worth every fucking tenner, and if you want to come outside now, I'll gladly have another hundred and twenty quid's worth.'

He didn't accept my offer, which was probably good news for both of us. The whole day had been such a downer. I lost the chance to meet the great Jimmy Cagney and gained a big dent in my wallet, all because of this wanker on a motorbike – and me to a certain extent, because I could've avoided it if I hadn't said anything when he nearly ran me over. As I've got older, I've learnt to avoid these kinds of situations much more effectively. It wasn't so much that I used to start trouble – in fact I don't think I've ever actively started a fight in my whole life – just that I wouldn't make that leap to trying to keep myself out of it.

'Attack is the best form of defence' – that's what I was taught – but really the best form of defence is not getting yourself in that position in the first place. Looking back on that incident with the biker now, I still think my dad and my granddad and his granddad before him (although then the messenger would've been riding a horse, not a motorbike) would have probably got in that fight, as well as all my mates and probably most of their wives.

When I look at my two older daughters I think, 'Yeah, probably them too.' But then I was still doing all this stuff when they were kids growing up, and it couldn't help but rub off on them. And hopefully now they're all out in the big wide world they're learning to do things differently. I've cleaned up my act a bit with my youngest, Ellie-Rae, so maybe she'll be the start of a new way of doing things.

Don't get me wrong, I still think you've got to stand up for what you believe in. I got in some funny situations when things weren't going too well as far as getting work was concerned and I certainly never regretted standing my ground in any of those.

Mike Leigh has never really been my cup of tea as a director. I like some of the stuff he's done, but it's the actors that make it – I just think he's a lucky fucker.

I went up for one of his things quite early on in my career and he was bombarding me with all these really strange questions. I wasn't ready for that because I didn't know him yet. I thought it was too early to be getting into such personal areas. I remember he asked me something about my dad and I said, 'What's my dad got to do with it? My dad ain't here.' Mike Leigh said, 'I'm just asking,' and I got a bit narky with him: 'Well, I don't want to answer that, alright?'

Then he told me he wanted me to 'find a character'. I said 'What character?' And he said, 'Make him up.'

At that point I got to my feet and walked out. I said I had to go to the toilet, but in fact I just fucked off home. They sent a message back later asking what had happened and I said, 'Ray's character wanted to go to the toilet, and then he wanted to fuck off home.'

The next person in after me that day was Mark Wingate who was in *Quadrophenia* with me. The story as I heard it was that Mike Leigh said, 'Shock me!' So Mark picked up the table in the room they were in and threw it out of the window. There was a rumour that the BBC made him pay for the damages, and if that was true then it was very wrong. If you're going to play that game, then you've got to follow through with it. You wanted to be shocked, and he fucking shocked you, so no one except you should be paying for any windows that got broken.

The Northern Irish actor Stephen Rea had a great victory over Mike Leigh by all accounts. Mike Leigh was following him down the road like he does when he's getting you to do things and Stephen went into a pub. Mike Leigh crept in after him and hid under a table – all the usual bollocks was going on. But then Stephen came on the screen in a film that was showing on the pub TV. So he looked across at where Mike Leigh was hiding and called out, 'Look, Mike, I'm on the telly!' I don't think he got the job either.

Another meeting I didn't get any work out of was with Steven Berkoff. It was for his play *West*, which he'd already done once and it was apparently quite famous, although I didn't know too much about it at the time. The idea was for it to be a kind of tongue-in-cheek cockney Shakespeare, but quite surreal, and our first meeting was certainly surreal enough. I know Steven now and I like him, but it would be true to say we didn't quite hit it off at first.

He's standing there with some kind of jump-suit on, all zipped up to the top and his big dot in the middle of his forehead, rolling his Rs when he talks to me and going, 'Rrrraymond-ah . . . I loved the way you walked across the room.' So I go, 'What do you want me to do then, mate?' And he says, 'I want you to walk in the bar and you're looking for someone.'

It's all that kind of broad caricature stuff he wants me to do, but I don't know that at the time. So I walk into this pub in my normal unobtrusive kind of way and just stand at the bar very quiet and not looking at anyone. Steven bellows, 'Stop! What are you doing?' and I say, 'I'm looking for someone.'

Steven says, 'But you haven't looked,' and I say, 'Exactly. When you're looking for someone, Steven, you don't look for someone. If I come in a pub and start looking around, they'll all know what I'm doing.' He's getting exasperated now: 'But I want you to look!'

So that was another job I didn't get. A fella I knew at the time called Ken did it in the end, and when I went to see the play the penny finally dropped. 'Oh, fuck me,' I thought to myself. 'That's what it's all about.' It was good, it was funny, but I'd thought it was a drama when it was actually more like a panto. Over time I've had to learn when to use what I got from Clarkey in terms of always trying to make things as real as possible, and when not to use it. Sometimes you might be doing something that's in a completely different genre where playing it for real is not the best way to go. Asking yourself, 'But how would I feel about this?' isn't something you necessarily need to do if you're in a musical.

It took me a few years to learn that, and it took me a few years to learn some other things as well. Drink-driving was another old habit that died hard. One time when I was still living up North I came home for the weekend and borrowed my sister's car to go out for the evening with my mate Tony Yeates. That car had holes in the floor – it was like something Fred Flintstone would drive.

We'd had a few drinks on Mare Street and when I stopped at the lights, a cop car pulled up alongside. What I tended to do in that situation – especially if I didn't have a seatbelt on – would be look the policeman straight in the eye as if to say, 'Hello, how are you?' So they don't think you're hiding something.

This time it was an old sergeant with a younger cop alongside him. I was a bit pissed and we didn't have seatbelts on, so I did the old 'hello' stare and the older copper kind of nodded, so that was going OK. Unfortunately, as I went to pull away, I stalled the car and by the time I'd got the engine started, they'd slowed down. I went up the side of them and fronted 'em out, but the damage was done. They pulled us over round the corner of Well Street – right outside Granddad's flat – and wallop, they were on us.

Me and Tony had this ploy where if we were ever going to get arrested, we'd always give each other's name. I'd be Tony Yeates and he'd be Ray Winstone – we'd swap birthdays and everything. Then if they get me to court as Tony Yeates, I can just say, 'No, that's not me.'

We're doing that when they get us out of the car. The young constable is about our age – early twenties – and he badly wants to nick us. I blow in the breathalyser bag as Tony Yeates and he's going, 'Blow in it properly.' When it makes the noise that means you're nicked, I can almost hear Tony going, 'Oh thank you very fucking much', under his breath.

Because I can see we're not going to get any joy out of the kid, I start talking to the old sergeant. I say 'old' but he's not walking with a stick, in fact he's probably in his thirties. His name is Alan, and as I'm explaining what's happened, I can already see he's a blinding fella. My story's basically true, which always helps. I'm telling him, 'Look, Sergeant, I don't live here at the moment, because I've moved to Manchester. But I've come down for the weekend and I've borrowed my sister's car to visit a mate I've not seen in years.' That was where the only slight element of exaggeration came in. 'We got on it and we've taken a bit of a liberty but we're home now – I'm staying up in those flats with my granddad – and we certainly won't be driving again tonight.'

Anyway, we have a good old chat, and because his mate is so hell-bent on nicking us, Alan decides to show him that there's a different way of doing things. So he deliberately breaks the breathalyser bag

and says, 'If I ever fucking catch you boozed up round here again ...'
I say, 'Oh thank you very much, Sergeant', and off we went.

Cut to about three years later. Me and Phil Daniels – who is a
terrible goalhanger by the way – are playing charity football against
the Old Bill at a police ground up on the North Circular, near
where Walthamstow dog track used to be. I think Tony Yeates has
come up to watch, just to complete the circle, and as I'm sitting there
having a fag as part of my half-time fitness regime, this copper comes
up and says, 'I know you, don't I?'

'Not me, mate' is the standard answer to give a policeman in that
situation, but Sergeant Alan isn't having it. He says, 'I breathalysed
you in Well Street, and your name ain't Yeates, is it?' From that point
on, we became really good mates. I used to do a lot of charity football for him out by Chadwell Heath. Alan ended up going into the
special armed services and he does security now. His boy joined the
force as well and he used to play against us. He was a lovely kid who
sadly got cancer and passed away, but not before we did a few charity
things for him as well.

When you look at how this whole situation developed, Alan gave
me a chance, so I gave him one too. If you'd asked me if I'd ever liked
a copper before I met him, the answer would be no. But what he did
for me changed my whole perception of the Old Bill. I wish I could
say it rehabilitated me on the drink-driving front too, but there were
a couple more incidents later on before I threw in the towel as far as
that was concerned.

The first one I was unlucky on. It was another charity football
match, this time out at Hungerford in Berkshire. Terry Marsh, the
former welterweight world champion, was meant to be driving us.
Now Terry is a great guy to drive you because he doesn't drink. That
whole thing where he was accused of shooting the promoter Frankie

Warren is something I would never ask him about. I don't want to know and it's not my business, but all I would say is that Terry had been a marine and I don't think someone with that training would have used a .22 to try and kill someone from that distance.

Anyway, I got a bit pissed at the do after the game, and suddenly started to worry that Terry had gone without me, so I jumped in another car to catch him up and tell him, 'You're meant to be taking us home.' Obviously, that wasn't the smartest or most logical decision I've ever made in my life, especially as I came round a corner and nearly hit a police car. In a country lane – what were the chances? By the time one of the coppers had opened the door and I'd fallen out onto the road, it's fair to say my fate was sealed. To make matters worse I found out afterwards that Terry was at the do all along and when the time came to leave he'd been wandering around looking for me.

You'd think this embarrassing incident would've done it for me, but no, I needed one more lucky escape. The day after I got my driving licence back, I was out at Worley Park playing golf when I got the hump at someone and stormed off home pissed. Then I took the wrong turn and ended up going down the M11. I was lucky I didn't have time to kill someone before I got collared and banged up in Epping police station. Talk about three strikes and you're out! It took me two convictions and someone giving me a chance before I finally got the message, but I've never done it since.

You couldn't drink and drive these days, anyway. There are too many idiots on the road.

CHAPTER 24

TROSSACHS, BARKING ROAD

It wasn't just my grasp of road safety that left a lot to be desired in the early eighties, I had plenty to learn about married life as well. I thought holy matrimony just meant the woman staying at home to cook the dinner while the man goes out to meet his mates. In my defence, all that New Man bollocks was still a long way off yet.

To be honest, I probably wasn't the greatest husband in the world. I was away a lot – not always getting arrested, only sometimes – and we both took a while to find our feet. It was tough. But Elaine never moaned about it when the money ran out. She's not one of those wives who'd say, 'It's all gone pear-shaped – you need to go out and get a normal job.' We never had that conversation.

She's always been very supportive when it's come to my acting. Her approach was: 'Whatever you wanna do, babe, however you wanna go about it.' Not that she was a soft touch – far from it – but I think because I was already doing what I was doing when she first met me, she understood that this was the way things were gonna be.

She's quite arty herself, and I think she knew she'd got herself an artful one from the beginning.

Elaine certainly did her bit when we were stuck up in Manchester without a pot to piss in. She'd make curtains for people or do a bit of interior designing for anyone who had the money to pay for it. And the food parcels from her mum down the road came in handy too, although I didn't like to admit that at the time.

By the time we'd had a couple of years of this, I think she was as fed up with it as I was. And the fact that we'd never really got around to keeping up the payments on our mortgage was inevitably going to bite us on the arse at some stage.

At one point we got a very welcome cheque through for some residuals – probably from *Fox*. It was five grand or something like that, which was a lot of money in those days, especially to people in our situation. I looked at Elaine and said, 'We've got two choices here – we can either pay the bills or go on holiday.' She asked me what I wanted to do and I said, 'Let's go on holiday.'

So we went away for a few weeks – I can't actually even remember where to, that's how much we enjoyed ourselves. By the time we got back we'd knocked out the five grand and I knew we were done as far as that house was concerned. The mortgage company said, 'We're gonna take your house from you and we're gonna sell it.' So I replied, 'I'll tell you what we're gonna do. I'm gonna give you the house – you're not gonna take it – and then I'm fucking off. How's that?'

They probably had a nice earner out of it in the end, and we were both ready to give it another go down south. It was either that or starve. Elaine's mum couldn't keep feeding and watering us forever. So we packed up what stuff we had and headed off back down the M6 (the right way this time, because Elaine wasn't driving).

Coming back to London was tricky at first because we had to go back and live at my mum and dad's for a few months to get ourselves sorted. It was really good of them to have us, but it was impossible living there as a married couple. My mum looked after us really well but Elaine wanted to be her own woman and the tension in the kitchen was horrible. I wasn't exactly jumping for joy about getting bossed around by my Old Man again either.

Luckily for everyone's blood pressure, my mum had taken the precaution of putting me on the council housing list in Enfield when I first went up to Manchester. I'd asked her why she'd done that at the time and she said, 'Because I know what you're like.' Maybe that wasn't the greatest vote of confidence, but it turned out Mum knew best, especially as Elaine was pregnant by this time.

There was nothing doing in housing terms at first, but we kept on going up the housing office until finally they gave us a maisonette at a rent we could almost afford. We were lucky to be part of probably the last generation where having a single child could still get you a council house somewhere near your family home – you didn't need to have one-legged triplets and an Arts Council grant yet. Once Maggie Thatcher sold all the council places off, some people made a lot of money, some more people got absolutely stitched up, and the lives of future generations got a lot more difficult.

I didn't see as much of the inside of that maisonette as I might've done in the early years of my lovely little Lois's life, because I was still what you'd call a going-out dad. (What would being a stay-at-home dad even mean? Being indoors all day and doing fuck all?) And the kind of places I used to go out to still weren't exactly domesticated. There was a pub called Trossachs on Barking Road which went through a few name-changes – always a sign of somewhere with a reputation to shake off. A lot of pubs and clubs did as the eighties progressed but there weren't many that could hold their hands up to calling themselves a hat-trick of Raffles, Valentino's and Memory Lane at one time or another.

Now that I think about it, I'm not absolutely certain the following incident did take place in Trossachs, but it's the kind of thing you're generally best advised not to be too specific about, so let's say it did. I was in there or somewhere very like it one night when a fella walked in wearing motorbike leathers and a crash-helmet and carrying a shotgun. The place was packed, and I guarantee you seventy-five per cent of the geezers drinking in that pub thought he was there for them. People were diving over the bar, under the tables, glasses were going everywhere. Some guys even put their birds in front of them, which probably didn't win them any prizes for chivalry afterwards. Saddam Hussein hadn't pioneered his human shields yet, so maybe this was where he got the idea.

The guy with the shotgun looked all around the gaff and obviously the geezer or bird he wants ain't in there – either that or he can't see them through the helmet. But he still wants to make an impression, so he shoots the carpet – bang! A big hole right there at his feet, and just walks out. At this point everyone slowly comes out from their hiding places, and the only one not joining in the collective sigh of relief is the guv'nor of the pub: 'Look what he's done to my fucking carpet!'

The carpets back at the maisonette in Enfield might not have got bullet holes in them, but the place did need a bit of a touch-up. And before that could happen I had to find a way of putting some food on the table. Luckily, a message that came to me via Don Boyd seemed to offer the prospect of some much-needed acting work. It was a big part, but there were some strings attached, as the phone-call came from a guy called Joey Pyle who was quite a major underworld face (although he denied everything till the day he died).

I ended up becoming a great friend of Joey's, and I still know his son today – little Joey Pyle Jnr – but at the time his was a name that made people (me included) very nervous. And when he told me they wanted me to play Ronnie Kray in a film Don Boyd had more or less ready to go, the stage was set for me to renew acquaintances with the man I had rather tactlessly pissed all over a quarter of a century before.

I didn't know where they'd got the idea of me playing the part from, because the twins certainly hadn't seen my *Trojan Women*. It was possible the idea had come from an old mate of my dad's called Laurie O'Leary, who was the only person I could think of who knew both them and me.

Sure enough, when the meet finally happens, Laurie is one of the men in the car that picks me up. He sits on one side of me in the back, with the intimidating figure of Joey Pile on the other. Talk about a rose between two thorns! In the passenger seat is a guy called Alex Steene, who I've never met before, but I know by his formidable reputation. The car's being driven by an old fighter called Alex Buxton, who'd boxed a world champion called Randolph Turpin years before.

Alex Buxton is a lovely man, and him being at the wheel gives the whole trip an extra layer of grandeur, not that it really needs it. No one really tells me where we're going at first, so I'm thinking, 'Who the fuck have I upset now?' Then as it slowly dawns on me that we're heading out into the country in the general direction of Broadmoor, I get more and more sucked into the drama of the whole thing.

It's almost like we were going to meet folklore – this terrifying character who was one of the great gangsters of all time. That's certainly how I'd have seen it when I was younger, and although I'd developed a bit more of a balanced perspective by the time all this was happening, it wouldn't have been a good idea to let Joey or Alex Steene see me taking the whole thing too lightly.

So even as I'm having a laugh with Laurie O'Leary, I'm being careful not to let anyone think I'm too relaxed. I'm also bearing in mind that it is a nuthouse we're drawing nearer to. And not just any nuthouse, but one that's full of sex offenders and murderers. What do I want to be going there for?

Once we've arrived and are going through all the rigmarole of getting in, I'm thinking, 'In an ideal world we'll be out of here in a few hours, because an overnight stay doesn't really appeal.' In a normal nick you're surrounded by people who've stolen a car or got pissed and hurt someone. In Broadmoor you're in there with people responsible for some of the most heinous crimes in history.

Every now and then you forget where you are, because it feels more like a hospital than a prison, but then you remember again. There's one kid serving the tea who it transpires has murdered his entire family. You're thinking, 'How did he kill his family again? Not that it's any of my business, but, just as a matter of interest, was it poison?' It's all very English in a way – sitting in a public place having a cuppa while trying not to mention the terrible things everyone around you has done.

One of the big questions on my mind when it comes to my re-acquaintance with Ronnie Kray is whether he is going to remember our earlier meeting. He does – either because he's been primed to remember it by Laurie, or because it's stuck in his mind for some other reason. I can't imagine he got pissed on too many times in his life (at least, not in company), and he makes a little joke about it as I arrive, which puts me more at my ease.

Ronnie is very smartly dressed, and looks well in himself, but he's quite a frail man at this stage in his life. He's not the same person you would've met on the outside fifteen years before, and you don't know what medication he's on, but there's still no mistaking the force of his personality. He doesn't just look at you, he looks straight through you to the wall behind, and his eyes have that kind of blankness where you feel you can't lie because he knows everything you're going to say before you actually say it, anyway. The only other time in my life I'd encounter a stare like that would be a few years later at Lewis Collins' house, where I met a few of the real-life SAS boys at a party for the film *Who Dares Wins*.

There are a couple of additional factors Ronnie is bringing to the table in terms of how intimidating a presence he is. First, he hangs on every word you say with an intensity that you never come across in normal people. Second, he sits very close to you so that his leg is rubbing against yours, and his leg does not keep still – it's constantly moving back and forth, almost like there's a twitch in it.

From the moment I've sat down he starts talking to me about Bob Hoskins, who I haven't yet met at the time. Ronnie's telling me about this play he's heard Bob's doing at a pub-theatre somewhere in South London. He says, 'Do you know this fella, Bob Hoskins?' His voice is a little bit nasal – almost like he's got a peg on his nose. I say, 'I know of him, Ron. He's just done the film *The Long Good Friday*.'

Ronnie nods. 'Well, he's been playing me in this play,' he continues. 'And this play implies I have incestuous feelings towards my mother.'

Ronnie doesn't swear very much, if at all, in conversation, because he's old-fashioned like that, so when he pauses for a moment and then asks, 'Is it a fucking crime to love your mother?', it's important to take him very seriously indeed. 'No, Ron,' I reply solemnly. 'It's not a crime to love your mother.'

You can see how angry he is about the whole thing. At this point he starts whispering something to one of the other fellas and I'm getting a bit concerned about the implications for a fellow professional. So I say, 'Let me tell you something, Ron. Bob Hoskins doesn't know you. Bob Hoskins is an actor who plays what's written in the script as close as he can to the way the director wants it. So it's not Bob's fault if there's something in the play that you don't like.' At this point Ronnie goes, 'Right, so who's the writer?' So now I've taken the heat off Bob and put it on a couple of other people without meaning to.

Nothing happened to them in the end, so presumably Ronnie thought better of it, but this wasn't the last time that day I'd inadvertently end up putting someone else in the frame. One of Ron's more upbeat topics of conversation was telling me about how when he got out he was going to go on a round-the-world cruise. Whether he meant that last word in both its usual senses Ronnie didn't make clear, but he did announce – leg twitching particularly forcefully at this point – that he was planning to take me with him.

I didn't think this was too good an idea for obvious reasons, but because I was still excited about the fact that this film seemed to be happening, I did mention a mate of mine who I thought might be good for a part in it: 'You know the family, Ron. It's Terry Murphy's boy, Glenn Murphy.' My old mate Glenn from the Repton was getting started as an actor around that time, and I knew he'd be perfect for the film, but afterwards I realised I had kind of dropped him in it. He's a good-looking man, Murph, and I think he did have a meet with Ronnie in the end which proceeded along very similar lines. There's not too much else to do in Broadmoor, after all, so talking to actors must've been a distraction. Our conversation was reasonably amicable apart from the leg thing and the Bob Hoskins thing (which I enjoyed telling Bob about years later – there was a smile on his face at the time, but you could see the cold air hitting the back of his neck). I was watching and listening to Ronnie very closely to prepare myself for the role, and the thing that most struck me about him was how different he was to the way people normally portray gangsters. His voice had that kind of old London sound to it where you could almost feel his mouth making shapes around the words.

Another person I ended up spending a fair bit of time with who talked like that was Bruce Reynolds, the mastermind behind the Great Train Robbery. He was an absolute gent, but I think I'd better save that story for another time.

As the Krays film got closer to getting the green light – I was gon-na play both Ronnie and Reggie by that time, with the whole thing being done in split screen – Don Boyd also put me in touch with the Krays' mum, Violet. She'd moved out of the house on Vallance Road by then and into some flats at the back of the Repton. I had a really good day with her and she gave me some blinding photos, which I sadly can't find, of the twins with Billy Hill, who was an early face from Brighton Races. As far as Violet was concerned, she was just a normal East End mum and they were her boys. She didn't really want to think too much about all the people they'd hurt or killed.

The Krays film didn't happen in the end. Well, it did, but in an-other form. I think there were some financial complexities of some kind and the project changed hands. Ray Burdis from the Anna Scher mob took it over and he wanted it to go in a more glamorous direction, so he cast the Kemp brothers instead of me. I had no regrets about it – these things happen and I actually thought the two Spandau Ballet boys did a blinding job in the end.

I didn't come out of that Broadmoor trip empty-handed either. I'd hit it off quite well with Alex Steene, and when the film didn't happen he asked me, 'Do you need a few quid, son, because work's not that good at the moment? Come up West and answer the phone for me.' At this point, given that you're talking to someone who's a very well-respected face, you're wondering what the fuck you might be getting yourself into. But it turned out to be a straight business, albeit a straight business that I always thought would make a great sitcom.

Alex's set-up was called The Unobtainables, and they were essentially high-class ticket touts. They traded out of an office in Panton Street, just near Leicester Square, selling city debentures at Wimbledon or the best seats at the rugby.

Anything you wanted The Unobtainables – as the name suggested – could get, and they'd pay a good price to get it as well. The ticket justified the means. Alex gave me a desk and a phone, and I soon found that I was pretty good at it. Basically it was the same thing I'd done on the markets – buying and selling commodities – only this time you were dressed a bit smarter, and there was less chance of being hit on the head with a flying cauliflower.

What I liked about working there was that you weren't hurting anyone. You were giving people something they wanted, and if they could afford to pay the money you were asking, that was up to them. Most of the clients were big companies in the City who were writing it all off, anyway. It was getting towards the mid-eighties by then, and there was a bit more money around.

The really funny thing about the job was the other people who worked there. As well as me, we had a couple of other actors. First there was Patrick Holt, a tall veteran of the Rank era who also played one of the old boys in the Roger Moore film, *The Sea Wolves*. He was a lovely stylish fella, very well spoken – in fact I once remember him telling me, 'You could've been my batman during the war'. He also gave us a fantastic recipe for goulash, which Elaine still cooks to this day.

Then there was Derren Nesbitt, who'd been quite a big star in the sixties and seventies, and played the sadistic SS officer in *Where Eagles Dare*. But the guv'nor when it came to selling tickets was a guy called Michael, who'd never acted in anything. He loved a drink so much that one night he went out for a beer in the West End and woke up on a boat in Norway. We had murders trying to get him back that day because there was a big deal depending on him. It was quite a high-pressure job in a way, because if you fucked up you knew who you had to deal with.

One day, a load of police swarmed the office. They were top-level Old Bill from Scotland Yard, and I assumed it was nothing to do with The Unobtainables because we were all working in the other room and we never got touched. But when I poked my head round the door to see what had happened, I found out that someone had sold two tickets for the Trooping of the Colour that were right next to where John Nott was going to sit. Given that he was Margaret Thatcher's Secretary of State for Defence at the time, this was a major security breach.

All they wanted to know was who had sold the tickets, but no one would admit to it, so I put my hand up and said, 'I did it', even though I didn't know if I had or not. The police said, 'Who are you?' And I said, 'Alex rents me the office next door and I do a bit of buying and selling for him.' When they asked me who I bought them off I just said, 'A couple of geezers came in. I didn't know who they were.' It turned out that it had been a couple of soldiers who'd come in with the tickets hoping to make a few quid, but it wasn't me they'd sold them to.

Alex's other business interests did sometimes make their presence felt in Panton Street. He was a Yorkshireman who was known for his tact and discretion, so that marked him out from the crowd for a start. And he was so good at not so much sitting on the fence as bringing people together that his office functioned almost like a relationship counselling service for London's biggest faces. He'd summon all the different firms to try and stop things getting nasty when there was a difference of opinion. It was fascinating to watch him in action, but sometimes when I'd hear Alex calling 'Ray-mond', because he wanted me to sit in on one of those meetings, I'd think, 'I'd rather not, thanks.' If it all went pear-shaped, I might end up being the patsy.

Sometimes you'd feel like you needed a blue helmet from the UN just to go into work. Notorious adversaries like the Richardsons from South London and Johnny Nash from North London would come in and sit round his table together. The interesting thing was that on the face of it, nobody wanted a row. Everything seemed to get resolved and they'd all shake hands at the end, but you'd never be quite sure if the handshake was proper or not.

These guys were the last of the old guard by that time – a lot of them had done their bit of porridge, and all they were after was a quiet life. It was the younger fellas coming through who'd tend to be more hot-headed and throw threats around, and the carnage you'd hear about in later years suggested that Alex's softly-softly way of reconciling gangland factions might have died with him.

CHAPTER 25

THE APOLLO STEAKHOUSE, STRATFORD

One of the best trips I ever went on for The Unobtainables was to Salzburg in Austria, where they filmed *The Sound of Music*. Alex wanted me to get tickets for a Leonard Bernstein concert for some geezers in the City. So I flew out there all suited up with twenty large distributed in various different pockets and set up a meet with the concierge of one of the best hotels in town. I've always had this feeling that if you really look after a top-notch concierge, he can probably sort you out with pretty much anything you want. So it proved on this occasion, as I gave him his bit of dough and he got me twenty prime tickets for the opening night, all at face value, which was a touch.

It was very *The Third Man* – swapping envelopes on the continent – and I got back to London expecting Alex to be ecstatic, which he was. I was waiting for him to give me my drink, or whatever other kind of bonus he thought was appropriate. It never came and it never came, until eventually he tried to slip me a measly few quid. I said, 'I think you'd better keep that, Alex. You probably need it more than me.' I suppose it was just that old face's mentality of 'Give someone just enough and they need to come back, give them too much and they'll be gone.' But whatever the reason, it was point taken at my end.

As it happened, the dates I'd been given were wrong, and that's why I'd been able to buy the tickets so easily. Luckily, it was the City boys' fault not mine, so there was a bit of a scream-up about that and everyone went potty back at the office. That's not the point of the story, though.

The thing I'll never forget about that Salzburg trip were these Hare Krishna geezers who were talking to me in this park where I was waiting to see the concierge. I'll have a chat with anyone when I'm bored, and they were nice enough people. They were trying to sell me their way of life – saying I'd never want for anything if I joined them – and I was smiling to myself thinking, 'I've got twenty large in my pockets. How much cash can that robe hold?'

I don't know if what they were telling me about reincarnation got in my head – the same way that thing my mate at school told me about the tape rewinding did – but I had a really strange moment of *déja vu* as I walked around the corner out of that park. It was almost like I knew where everything was going to be before I'd even got there . . . This clock on the right, that shop on the left . . . I'd never visited the place, but I knew exactly where everything was. The only rational explanation I could come up with afterwards was that it was a location I remembered from *The Sound of Music*.

When I was a kid watching films like that one or *Lawrence of Arabia* or *Bridge on the River Kwai* on the big screen, I never dreamed I'd be up there myself one day. Sometimes it can be disappointing when you come across the people who've made the movies you've loved in real life. I met the director David Lean (the man behind those last two films) early on in my career when he was gonna do *Mutiny on the Bounty*. I normally get on well with directors, but he was quite a rude man.

You know as soon as you walk into the room whether they want you or not, and it was plain he didn't like the cut of my jib, but I persisted because I was such a fan of the things he'd done in the past. I asked him, 'What's this one all about then, David?' He said, 'Why do you want to know?' So I told him how much I'd loved his work and that I was really interested in what he was going to do this time round, but he just didn't want anything to do with me.

The only thing that made me feel better about it was a few years later when I went to a talk Alec Guinness gave in a small room at the Young Vic. Guinness had been in a lot of Lean's films so I asked him what he thought of him and he said, 'A wonderful film-maker, but what a horrible nasty man!' So it wasn't just me then ...

If you've grown up watching films starring the Alec Guinnesses and the Richard Burtons and the Peter O Toole's of this world, you can't help seeing that as the gold standard everyone should aim for. But then you look at yourself and you know you can't even speak the Queen's English. So you think, 'Well, how is that gonna work?' In the phase of my life when I was one of The Unobtainables, it still wasn't really working yet. In fact, I don't think I'd look at a performance I'd done and think it was good enough until *Nil by Mouth* more than fifteen years later.

But I was learning, however slowly. I saw a lot of things go down in those two years I worked for Alex Steene. That guy Alan Lake, who used to knock about with Diana Dors – he came in a lot. They really loved each other those two, and Alan was a blinding bloke – a bit of a nut-nut, but I did like him. He used to come in the office and do handstands. Anyway, a terrible thing happened one night when we all went down the Lyceum together. Diana was there – she knew all the chaps and she was good friends with Alex. But when Alan walked in the room, the whole audience booed him. I never knew why – there must have been something in the papers – but those are the kind of things that stay with you.

It's weird the way people think at times. I was indoors at the maisonette in Enfield once (it did happen sometimes) when a policeman came round. He told me that a guy who'd attacked an old car-park attendant on the King's Road in Chelsea had claimed as part of his defence that he wasn't there because he was having a drink with Ray Winstone. I didn't even know the guy – he must've seen me in a film or on TV and thought, 'Oh, he'll vouch for me.' Like you're gonna vouch for a geezer who's beaten up some old car-park attendant, anyway!

It was a fucking joke – even the copper was laughing. I think he knew it was all cobblers. He was a nice copper, actually – I could accept that they existed now, thanks to Sergeant Alan. This was just one of those shock realisations which were dragging me kicking and screaming into the world of the adult. It's hard to look back and pick out one moment when you really started growing up. But I've got to do it, otherwise I can't really justify calling this book *Young Winstone* and finishing it before I become the international Hollywood love god who Matthew McConaughey knows and envies today.

I'm not one of those dads who'll tell you that they suddenly understood everything about the world the moment they had their first child. As I've said already, my approach to parenting as a younger man – certainly with my first daughter Lois, hopefully a bit less with Jaime – was more in line with that of an earlier generation. Mum's job is to be at home with the kids, while geezers go out and get the bread and butter then go to the pub because they've been working all week and they deserve it. The catch is, sometimes even if they haven't been working all week, they still go to the pub anyway.

I was still out and about a lot in East London. My eating place of choice – where I'd now go with Tony Yeates or some of the other boys – had graduated two stops down the Central Line from the Venus steakhouse in Bethnal Green to the Apollo in Stratford. Steakhouses often have classical-sounding names because they're usually run by Greek fellas, and Panny and Gilly, the two geezers who owned the Apollo, kept a blinding gaff. They did great grills and made lovely margaritas. You'd see all the East End glamour in the Venus over the years: Page 3 girls and West Ham's Frank McAvennie – old Mackers – he was a good mate of mine. There was a party atmosphere and the grub was great – we took Phil Daniels in there a few times, and Perry Fenwick who plays Billy Mitchell in *EastEnders*.

Given how keen I always was to be back in the East End as a teenager, I suppose it's strange I wasn't moving heaven and earth to persuade Elaine that we needed to live there. I'm not going to say East London had become a state of mind for me, because that would sound a bit poncey, but the sense of belonging which endured from my childhood there was definitely something I carried with me – off-screen and on: a kind of happiness, in a way.

It was important for me to have that, given that I was working in a business where I didn't always feel I belonged. And the sense of me being someone who knew who they were was probably something casting directors were picking up on once I started to get a bit more work. The ability to fully inhabit a place you don't actually live in is what acting's all about, after all.

I came out of the job with The Unobtainables to another regular gig, this time as Will Scarlett in the ITV series *Robin of Sherwood*. It lasted three years and was a big breakthrough in terms of knowing what I was doing and all-round professionalism. But some very serious things happened while I was going back and forth to Bristol playing one of Robin's Merrie Men, the kind of things that don't really leave you any other option than to grow up.

The first sucker punch was my mum getting cancer. She had it for two years before finally dying when she was fifty-two and I was twenty-eight. The reason cancer is such a very cruel disease is because it leads you down an alley of thinking, 'Oh, you look alright today, you look good – maybe you've turned a corner', but then you go round that corner and there the cancer is waiting for you again. I was looking at all these special diets for her and places she could go to maybe have another chance – even fucking faith-healing starts getting into your head because you will grab at any old twig in the hope that it might turn into an olive branch.

To be honest with you, I don't think I've ever got over my mum's death. You've got your five basic senses in life – smell, taste and the other three – but on top of that there's a more general sense of yourself and the place you occupy in the world. Some people get that from religion, but as far as I'm concerned it comes from the people you love and the people who love you. And that higher sense kind of went from me a bit for a few years after my mum died. I lost it, and I'm not sure I've fully got it back, even now, because the connection a person has with their mum is like no other. You're from your mum, you've come out of her; two thirds of our bodies are water, and it all flows in the same direction.

One thing that did help at the time was a great conversation I was able to have with Mum just before she died. We all hoped she was going to get better, but I think everyone knew deep down how unlikely that was, especially once she'd gone into a coma. I was away in Bristol at the time doing *Robin of Sherwood* and there was a big fight scene with Jason Connery coming up the next day. We'd designed it a bit like the one in *The Quiet Man* with John Wayne, and we were just going through the final preparations the night before when I had the thought that I needed to go home.

The producers were great about it – I'd told them this moment was going to come. So I raced back to London for the next day and found that my mum had come out of her coma. I sat and talked to her all day long. We had a great chat about my dad, about life in general. It was all the conversations you often end up wishing you could have but don't get the chance to.

My mum had always been very proud of me and backed me to do what I wanted in life (as did my dad, who might not have been easily impressed by musical theatre, but only ever wanted the best for me and my sister). She used to sit around with the aunties and watch me in *Scum*, which can't have been an easy thing for a mum in a way, but she always used to say, 'If that's what you want to do with your life, son, you go and do it.' Still, I think she'd realised that we needed to have a talk. It wasn't all in the past tense as if she knew she was about to die. She made the whole thing feel more natural than that, just like a general reassurance that everything was in place: 'Don't worry about your father, he'll be alright.' Lois can't have been more than eighteen months old at the time, so we talked about how much Mum loved her, and Elaine was pregnant with Jaime, so that was another good topic. And shortly after the conversation ended, Mum passed away.

We'd lost another child in between those two happy births, and Mum had still been alive when the baby boy died, so those two deaths came quite close together. Elaine was about seven months pregnant and the baby wasn't right, but she had to give birth, anyway. I was there with her through the delivery, and I can tell you it was hard. Those are the kinds of experiences that can destroy you if you let them.

I think what helped us through the aftermath was knowing that my mum and dad had been through the same experience. Their attitude was: 'It happens. You're not the only people in the world who have had to go through this, so the best thing is just to get on with it.' Now, while that's not necessarily what you want to hear at the time, it does liven you up a bit. It's like having Jackie Bowers in your corner.

We weren't really the sort of people who would sit down and talk to a counsellor or a psychiatrist. In a way, maybe we needed to, but they'd probably have fucked us up even more. So, following my mum and dad's stoic example was probably our best bet in the end, and the fact that Elaine fell pregnant again quite quickly afterwards with Jaime definitely helped.

It was a tough thing, but when a little bit of time has passed you've got to try and take positives out of those situations, and the way I've always looked at it is that if the other child had lived, we might not have had our Jaime, who we love. The upshot of all this is that I'm the last of the male line, as far as the Winstones are con-cerned. Lois and Jaime tell me they'll go double-barrelled when the time comes for them to get married, which is very decent of them, but they don't have to do it.

It was funny when all my three daughters were born. I was so caught up in the moment that I didn't even know if they were boys or girls for the first half-hour. It didn't worry me. I just had 'em in my arms and that was all that mattered. Of course, I would have liked to have had a boy – a son to carry on the family name. That would've been wonderful, but I suppose I did have one in a way, if only for a small amount of time.

Elaine and I would have loved to have held him in our arms too – just for a moment – but he was taken away before we got the chance. To be honest with you, I think two Young Winstones died that day. I'll never forget the one who didn't make it, and the pain of my son's passing marked the end of the person this book is about, and the beginning of whoever the older and maybe slightly wiser version was going to be.

PICTURE CREDITS